CONNECTING:
52 Guidelines for Making Marriage Work

CONNECTING:

52 Guidelines for Making Marriage Work

Harold J. Sala

CHRISTIAN PUBLICATIONS, INC.
CAMP HILL, PENNSYLVANIA

ᯀCHRISTIAN PUBLICATIONS, INC.

3825 Hartzdale Drive, Camp Hill, PA 17011
www.christianpublications.com

Faithful, biblical publishing since 1883

Connecting: 52 Guidelines for Making Marriage Work
ISBN: 0-87509-929-7
LOC Control Number: 2001-134118
© 2002 by Harold J. Sala
All rights reserved.
Printed in the United States of America.

02 03 04 05 06   5 4 3 2 1

*Affectionately dedicated to the most wonderful
woman in the world, who has been by
my side for more than four decades.
My best friend, my confidante,
my encourager and prayer partner,
the wonderful mother of our three children,
my wife, Darlene.*

Contents

Part IV Infidelity and Your Marriage

Part V Men and Women Are Different

Part VI Balancing Marriage with the Demands of Life

Part VII Touching God for Your Marriage

Part VIII Building for Tomorrow

Preface

An acquaintance of mine tells about the time he was on a plane and noticed that the fellow sitting next to him wore his wedding ring on his middle finger. While that is the accepted practice in some cultures, most people—at least in the West—wear their wedding rings on the fourth finger of their left hand, a practice which stems from an old belief going back to Roman days that a vein went from this finger directly to the heart.

"You know," said the friend, "it's really none of my business, but I noticed that your wedding ring is on *the wrong finger!*"

"Yep," said the stranger, "as a matter of fact, I married *the wrong girl* too!"

More than a few people have thought that about their spouse. After the initial romance of the marriage wears off (which is usually within the first two years) and hard, cold reality sets in, a person may wake up and say, "I've made a big mistake! This is not the person that I thought I was marrying!" Right then a fork in the road looms up with far-reaching consequences. The person asks, "Do I stay in this marriage and try to make the best of a not-so-great situation, or do I do what so many do—bail out and try again?" This dilemma can be intensified by the realization that God doesn't approve of divorce, so the frustration of unhappiness is compounded and can be downright depressing.

So it would seem that one of two things is true. Either God has a rather warped sense of humor, expecting His children to stay in not-so-good marriages knowing that we would be miserable and unhappy, or else He has a way for us to confront issues, learn how to communicate, resolve conflict and cope.

It is possible for two people—even if they are about as different as daylight and dark—to make sunshine together because we have the quiet, regenerating power of the Holy Spirit at work in our lives.

My wife and I stood at the confluence of the Danube and Ems Rivers in Austria and noticed that as the two great rivers came together there was a vast amount of turbulence, yet downstream a few kilometers the waters flowed smoothly. I couldn't help thinking that when two people come together in marriage, they are much like two great rivers that merge: it is to be expected that there should be turbulence. Marriage is a blending of habits, personalities, backgrounds, idiosyncrasies of temperament and DNA—a powerful mixture. Along with that there may also be the conflict of two cultures or the challenge of a blended family (his kids and her kids).

Darlene and I understand that because our two families were about as different as two families could be. I'm from a long line of extroverts. Suffering in silence was not done in the household in which I grew up. If something was on our minds, we said so—often in quite loud and expressive terms.

My wife, however, was the only child born to a mother whose background was Canadian and a wonderful dad whose polite reserve made it extremely difficult for him to assert himself even when people took advantage of him. If someone were standing on Pop's foot in a crowded bus, it would have been difficult, if not downright impossible, for him to tell the guy to "move it!"

They were a physical contrast as well. Pop was six-feet-two-inches tall and weighed about 250 pounds while

Momma was about four-feet-eight-inches tall and weighed less than eighty pounds, dripping wet. But never forget that dynamite comes in small packages.

In my wife's family nonverbal communication was an art form. If Olympic medals were given in nonverbal communication, my mother-in-law would have been a strong contender for the gold. When she sniffed, Pop knew the cue and immediately jumped to the task. When we began to date and our relationship deepened, Darlene would sniff (much as her mother had done) and I would hand her a handkerchief! I didn't get it. I didn't have the foggiest notion of what was going on, and she wouldn't tell me either.

After almost three years of what I thought was a blissful courtship, I drove to California where she was vacationing with her parents, prepared to give her a diamond and ask her to marry me and live happily ever after.

After dinner at a Laguna Beach restaurant, I happened to find a scenic spot where the moonlight filtered through the clouds over the beautiful Pacific, and—you guessed it—asked her to marry me.

About all she could do was cry and try to tell me why she couldn't marry me. It was the lowest moment of my life. Later that night I opened my Bible to Hebrews 12 and read where God disciplines those whom He loves. We later compared notes, and I found out that that same night, Darlene had opened her Bible to Proverbs 3, which says the same thing. (Note: Hebrews 12 quotes the passage found in Proverbs.)

The problem in our relationship was a severe lack of communication. Thankfully, Darlene had the wisdom to know that if we didn't communicate before marriage, putting wedding rings on our fingers wouldn't cause the light to come on!

Yes, I loved her and she loved me, but knowing that it takes more than love to make a marriage work, she felt that the problems we would have faced would have been too great to provide much happiness. At that point it seemed we had no future. We stopped seeing each other and I took the engagement ring back to Cory's Jewelry Store and asked for a refund. I was wounded but didn't know what to do to fix the situation.

Then my twenty-seven-year-old sister died from lupus erythematosus, a degenerative blood disease of the connective tissues which can now be managed with steroids and new drugs. I was completely devastated. I cried. I hurt, and learning of my loss, Darlene sent her sympathies. I wanted to talk about it with her, and as Darlene and I talked, she saw the real me. Through sharing the loss of my sister we learned to let down the barriers and be vulnerable with each other. Darlene learned she could be totally honest and completely open with me and I would not only really listen but value her input as well.

The next time I asked her to be my wife, the situation was different. We knew each other. We could communicate. We could cry together, talk together and face life together. I went back to Cory's Jewelry Store and to my great elation repurchased the same ring. That ring has been on the fourth finger of my wife's left hand now for more than four decades.

The longer a couple waits to learn how to communicate, to be vulnerable and to have a gut-level honesty with each other, the more painful and difficult it is to learn, but it is never too late.

For most of our married lives Darlene and I have been working with couples, many of whom found themselves in difficult marriages. We are convinced that with God's help anyone can make their marriage work. Walking out of a marriage when things get tough is not a solution and divorce is not a problem-solving technique.

The selections in this book were originally written for my radio program, *Guidelines for Living*, and are intended to generate discussion, thought and to serve as positive reinforcement for what you probably know you should do but don't.

My special thanks goes to my daughter, Nancy Deushane, along with Luisa Ampil, who spent many hours making corrections to this manuscript. Thanks also to Ed and Angie Wright who provided a quiet hideaway in the desert so I could work on this book.

May you *connect* with your spouse in a deeper and more meaningful relationship as the result of working through the selections in this book.

—Harold J. Sala

Part I

Going Back
to the Basics

"The difference between courtship and marriage is the difference between the picture in the seed catalog and what comes up."[1]
—James Wharton

A Recipe for Marriage

"For this reason a man will leave his father and mother and be united to his wife, and they will become one flesh." (Genesis 2:24)

Among the pool of memories I will always treasure is one of my grandmother's oatmeal cookies. I would go to my grandmother's house after having piano lessons at Mrs. Schuler's two doors down, and when I got there a platter of delicious oatmeal cookies would be waiting for me. After Darlene and I married, I asked Grandma for the recipe. "Well," she said, "you take about a cup of oatmeal and a couple tablespoons of this, and a pinch of that" and so forth.

There was no written recipe, no precise measurement of ingredients. She simply had years of experience and knew what was necessary to produce cookies that were marvelous, batch after batch. A recipe for marriage is much like the one my grandmother had for oatmeal cookies. The success or failure depends entirely upon what you put into it and whether or not the correct amounts are used. Leave out an ingredient or use too little of it, and it's just not the same.

Let's take a look at marriage in terms of baking a batch of cookies. To develop a great recipe for marriage, we need to start with the mixing bowl of faith, which is foundational to all of the relationships that take place in a home. It's a proven fact—leave God out of your marriage and you're headed for trouble.

The first ingredient that goes into the marriage mixing bowl of faith is the flour of commitment. Nothing is more basic to baking than flour, and in marriage nothing is more fundamental and important than commitment. Sadly lacking in many marriages is the "till death us do part" kind of commitment that is pledged at a marriage altar. Commitment means "God brought us together, and come hell or high water, someway, somehow, we're going to get through this problem!"

It's a proven fact—leave God out of your marriage and you're headed for trouble.

To the flour of commitment we add the oil of communication. Effective communication is the mutual exchange of ideas, thoughts, attitudes, information and feelings. It is a prerequisite to real love, and without it love withers and dies. Before a person can truly love another person, he must get to know that person, and if they don't communicate, there is no way that is going to happen. Therefore, without communication, there is no chance for love to grow. Get the picture? Commitment precedes love because if you're not committed to a marriage, then when difficulties come, you don't care enough to try to communicate.

Next add the sugar of love. Though we talk much about love, it is a difficult thing to define. It is better understood when you are on the receiving end of this commitment to care. It may be a difficult concept to grasp, but it is an essential ingredient in the recipe of a good marriage.

Another ingredient that allows both marriages and cookies to come out successfully is the baking powder of forgiveness. Leave baking powder out of most cookies, and you have tough, flat little wafers. Similarly, without a measure of forgiveness in a marriage it is apt to collapse

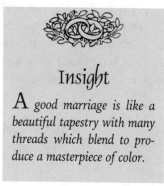

Insight

A *good marriage is like a beautiful tapestry with many threads which blend to produce a masterpiece of color.*

in times of stress. Simply put, forgiveness means "I give up my right to hurt you because you hurt me."

Now, add the eggs of meeting each other's needs. In baking, eggs bind the other recipe ingredients together. By meeting each other's needs in marriage, we bind ourselves closely together, keeping temptation away and adding joy to our relationship.

Another ingredient which needs to be added to the mixing bowl is the spice of humor. In baking we use salt, vanilla, cinnamon and other spices to make the cookies more flavorful. In marriage this spice can signify wholesome laughter—at ourselves, our failures and our foibles—and can add flavor and enjoyment to our relationship.

The final ingredient is frosting. We can think of the frosting as understanding, topping our marriage by putting our spouse first.

A final thought: None of these ingredients tastes very good separately, but mix them together and apply heat and you have something very, very good. Grandma's recipe works as well for marriages as it did for oatmeal cookies.

Think on This

1. All marriages face times of stress. In your marriage what things help you face difficult times?
2. What areas of your marriage need help?
3. How long has it been since you and your mate had a weekend together with no interruptions?

Resource Reading
Ephesians 5:17-25

Marrying Your Opposite

"Most of all, let love guide your life, for then the whole church will stay together in perfect harmony." (Colossians 3:14, LB)

Do opposites attract each other? You bet they do. That explains why an individual who never plans anything beyond his next meal ends up marrying a girl who is super organized, the kind who carries a small notebook with a to-do list of items a mile long. Some folks like rock music; others like classical. Some prefer to sleep with the windows open; others want them shut. Some squeeze the toothpaste in the middle of the tube; others roll the tube from the bottom.

Opposites may attract each other, but when there are too many dissimilarities, they may end up repelling each other, and that's when the fire flares.

How do we explain the fact that many people marry individuals who seem to be the exact opposite of themselves? The answer is that we marry to complete ourselves. Thus the organized person who wishes he or she were more of the free-spirited type is attracted to the opposite type of individual. And sometimes the sweet, virtuous and steady girl ends up marrying the guy who can't hold a job and won't darken the door of a church.

Marriage is not a win-lose situation, but an ongoing dialogue.

The question is: can two individuals who are almost opposites in personalities and sometimes backgrounds and/or cultures find happiness together? The answer: they can, provided they observe and practice the following guidelines.

Guideline #1: Respect each other's differences. There can be no real love apart from respect. When you really love someone you must be willing to accept the fact that you may not operate the same way as your spouse. Lots of differences in a relationship may add spice—and conflict—but there has to be a core of respect that can't be violated. Try this exercise to help you visualize this concept: draw two circles and then bring them toward each other until the two overlap. Each circle represents individual differences, but the core which overlaps is the area of mutual respect and tolerance. As Paul wrote to the Colossians, put up with one another in love, respecting what makes each of you who you are (see Colossians 3:13).

Guideline #2: Talk about it. Free and open communication is a must for a successful marriage. When taking the kids and climbing Mt. Shasta is more than you can handle, say so without attacking the other person. This means, of course, that somewhere in between there has to be a solution that keeps you both happy. Look for the solution rather than how to win the argument.

Guideline #3: Compromise. Marriage is not a win-lose situation, but an ongoing dialogue. Someone said that marriage consists of one "I do" followed by a lot of little "uh-huhs." Those little "uh-huhs" represent all of the compromises that come about as part of the continuing dialogue of a good marriage.

Guideline #4: Submit your differences to a higher court of appeals. Making Christ the head of your home supplies an atmosphere in which you are able to pray together. You can then openly ask the Lord for His help and direction in solving conflicts which come because of differences. When couples refuse to talk and pray about differences, they are in for a

Insight

Two individuals who are vastly different from each other can either be supremely happy together, or can be extremely unhappy together—it all depends on the focus of their relationship.

lot of conflict; but when two people—even two very different people—love each other and sincerely seek God's best for their lives and children, it is amazing how supremely happy they can become. In these types of relationships, individual differences complement each other rather than conflict with each other.

Yes, two people can be very different and yet very happy. That's a fact.

Think on This

1. Understand that what you so admired in your spouse may be the very quality to which you must adjust, so focus on making allowances for that personality type.

2. You will either compete with each other or complement each other. Making the application of these four
   guidelines a daily discipline will help you find the middle ground of common interests which will make for
   comfort in your relationship.

Resource Reading
Colossians 3:1-17

The World's Most Married Man

"The man who finds a wife finds a good thing; she is a blessing to him from the Lord." (Proverbs 18:22, LB)

He found a niche in the *Guinness Book of World Records* as the world's most married man, but when Glynn Wolfe died, not one of his wives cared enough even to bury him. The man who had a tattoo on his forearm of a tied knot had trouble keeping the marriage knot tied. Twenty-nine times Wolfe went to the altar, and he divorced the same number of times. But when he died, he was buried in a pauper's grave and not a single one of his former wives attended. Of his reported nineteen children and forty grandchildren, only one—a son who never got to know his father—was at the funeral. When the dirt covered the donated casket, a host of his descendants also hoped to cover their dark memories of the man and get on with their lives.

Surprisingly, newspapers and magazines picked up on the quaintness of a man who had married twenty-nine times and tried to contact some of his former wives. One paper said, "The man whose family tree sent branches and sub-branches into every direction, the man who married more often than Zsa Zsa Gabor, Elizabeth Taylor and Henry VIII combined, the man who made twenty-nine different till-death-do-us-part promises was singularly alone at the end."[2] The article had been captioned, "Most Married, but Little Missed."

A number of marriage and family therapists offered their comments, trying to explain how anyone could fail so miserably at relationships. They pointed out that a lot of lives were badly hurt in the wake of his matrimonial escapades.

Y*ou get out of marriage what you put into it, whether it is fulfillment, excitement, joy and happiness, or indifference, trouble and boredom.*

When he was once asked why he changed marriage partners so often, he replied that after a while he just got bored and wanted to find something new and exciting. It didn't work. He died almost broke, homeless and alone, with a wedding dress reportedly hanging in his closet, just in case he could find bride number thirty.

How sad! Yet the loneliness Glynn Wolfe experienced isn't much different from that which faces many other individuals—even those who have fame and lots of money. J. Paul Getty, once known as the richest man in the world, said he would gladly trade all his millions for just one lasting marital experience.

Glynn Wolfe was just plain sick, right? Few would disagree, yet I'm wondering what happiness he might have found had he followed the example of Henry Ford, who was once asked how he could stay married to the same woman for so many years. "I've treated marriage just like the automobiles I've built," said Ford, adding, "Just stick to one model."

Is sticking to one model boring? Not unless you are the bore. No matter how long you've been married, you can make your marriage unique, special and—though I hesitate to use the often overused and misused word—exciting.

You get out of a marriage what you put into it, whether it is fulfillment, excitement, joy and happiness, or indifference, trouble and boredom.

Insight

"We have met the enemy," says a line from a comic strip, "and he is us!"

Don't try to top the record of twenty-nine attempts at happiness. It doesn't come by changing partners but by being the partner you want the other to be. The real problem isn't the other person, but the one who looks back at you in the mirror. When he died, Wolfe left nothing but bad memories to his wives and children. The small inheritance he did have went to the stranger who ran the photocopy business where he took his divorce papers for reproduction.[3] Who can top that for being a loser!

Think on This

1. As you work through this book, take time to talk together as a couple. You may want to underline passages and take advantage of the opportunity to express yourself.
2. The resource readings are coordinated with the theme of each selection. To get the most out of this book,

take your Bible and read the Scripture along with the selection.

Resource Reading
Proverbs 31

When Commitment
Is Missing

"So Jacob served seven years to get Rachel, but they seemed like only a few days to him because of his love for her." (Genesis 29:20)

Someone defined a conservative as a liberal whose daughter has become a teenager. Strange, isn't it, that people who sowed their wild oats as teenagers are stronger disciplinarians and more cautious as parents than those who were less carefree in their youth?

In the 1960s Hugh Hefner launched the Playboy revolution, telling us that sex is a personal matter between consenting adults, that extramarital and premarital sex are OK provided two adults agree. From that beginning the fabric of marriage began to unravel. Eventually society came to accept cohabitation without marriage as the logical, if not inevitable, result of a relationship.

The 2000 U.S. Census documented the fact that in the '90s the number of unwed partners rose by an astounding seventy-two percent.[4] During the same decade researchers began to document the harsh reality that living together to see if you are good for each other is counterproductive to real happiness and long-term relationships.

Among the many studies which have been done on the subject of premarital cohabitation is a twenty-three-year research project by Professors William G. Axinn of the University of Chicago and Arland Thorton of the University of Michigan. The findings of those two sociologists show that the experience of setting up unmarried households "produces attitudes and values which increase the probability of divorce" by a factor of at least fifty percent.[5]

The emotional impact of bonding and the psychological closeness which results when two people give themselves to each other are missing from relationships outside of marriage. For women in particular this emotional bonding is powerful, and when the commitment of marriage is missing, a woman can feel used, cheapened and angry. Talk of love is meaningless without commitment.

God's purpose in prohibiting premarital sex in His Word is to spare us the heartache and loneliness of rejection and abandonment.

I'm thinking of a young couple I recently counseled. She was barely sixteen and he was only a few years older. Her father had abandoned her long ago, and her mother was an alcoholic who was glad to be rid of the responsibility of a teenager. They wanted to marry, and as I pressed the issue of maturity and what it takes to forge a lasting relationship, the young man said, "If we don't marry quickly, I can't help having a sexual relationship with her."

"Look," I said, "you aren't an animal. You are a human being created in the image of God, one who has a will."

But that's just the problem. When you are young and think that you are in love and your relationship becomes physical, you don't think of the implications or try to understand how you will view the other person in five or ten years.

Insight

W*hen God indicated that it was His plan for a man to leave father and mother and to be joined to his wife, thereby becoming one, it was not to restrict us but to complete us.*

Though most people tacitly recognize that morality and premarital abstinence are biblical values, they seldom recognize that God's plan for sexual relationships is the only thing that produces lasting happiness and permanence in relationships.

What the casual sex revolution never took into account is the emotional bonding which takes place in a sexual relationship, which is the glue that is meant to keep us together in difficult times as well as in good ones. But when there is no lasting commitment of marriage and a person chooses to walk away from a relationship, the fabric of the other person's life and soul may be ripped apart and loneliness and pain will fill an aching void within them.

Today the number of people who believe that having sexual relations apart from marriage is "always wrong" has declined to barely one-fourth of the adult population. Nonetheless, the gap between broken homes and lasting commitment continues to widen, a trend which cannot be lightly ignored.

What society believes isn't the issue. But what God said long ago regarding the commitment of marriage needs to be rediscovered. Why? It still works and still produces the joy and happiness a bride and groom expect as they stand starry-eyed at the marriage altar.

The lowered moral standards of society have not lowered the level of people's expectation of happiness. God's purpose in prohibiting premarital sex in His Word is to spare us the heartache and loneliness of rejection and abandonment. This principle doesn't just apply to biblical times; it is still true today.

Think on This

1. To what degree does the Playboy mentality influence the thinking of nominal Christians today?
2. Can you accept the fact that what God said regarding relationships stemmed from His knowledge that we can only find true fulfillment and happiness in an untarnished marriage relationship and that He never intended to limit our freedom or thwart our pleasure?

Resource Reading
Matthew 5:27-32

Commitment and What Counts in Life

"Whatever you do, work at it with all your heart, as working for the Lord, not for men, since you know that you will receive an inheritance from the Lord as a reward." (Colossians 3:23-24)

How would you rate the importance of commitment to a marriage? a) very important; b) moderately important; c) slightly important; or d) not important at all. If you say moderate to very, you're saying what the majority *says*, but if you rate it slightly to not important at all, you're where the majority of folks *live*.

A few years ago I did a series of programs on my *Guidelines* radio program and was talking about communication as being the most important key to resolving many of the problems in today's marriages. Responding to what I said, a listener wrote to me and said she agreed yet disagreed. She said there is something that goes deeper than communication: commitment! She's right, for without commitment a person doesn't care enough to communicate and without communication love withers and dies.

On the morning of a certain couple's wedding, my secretary overheard the bride turn to a bridesmaid and say, "Well, I'll give it a try, and if it does not work out, I can always divorce him and try again." That young woman had made the decision to marry, but she had not made a commitment to the one she was going to marry.

Commitment is a very important part of many aspects of our lives. It is vitally necessary in our vocations. Without a sense of commitment no individual will ever be successful in their job.

> ## I*t is high time we again learned that things which are worth having can only be purchased with the currency of commitment.*

There is another area where we need commitment and I believe that our failure to have it in this area automatically creates failure in our commitment to our marriages and our jobs. You guessed it—it is a lack of spiritual commitment. When you believe that God is alive and that your life, your marriage and work are not a matter of indifference with God, then His presence gives meaning to your existence. When you are spiritually committed, your work becomes more than a job; it becomes a ministry.

There is a great deal said in the Bible to this effect. For example, Paul urged the Colossians: "Whatever you do, work at it with all your heart, as working for the Lord, not for men, since you know that you will receive an inheritance from the Lord as a reward" (Colossians 3:23-24). And to the Corinthians he wrote, "So whether you eat or drink or whatever you do, do it all for the glory of God" (1 Corinthians 10:31).

I remember being in Portugal a number of years ago, and wherever I went I saw communist slogans and red, hand-painted hammers and sickles on walls, buildings and billboards. "Why don't they get rid of those?" I asked Sam Johnson, a missionary friend, and he replied,

Insight

Nothing of lasting value—your marriage, a cause worth fighting for, a job worth succeeding at—is attained without commitment.

"There's no way they can," explaining that the people who were responsible for the signs would sleep for a few hours, then hit the streets putting up political posters and then go to work for a full day. He said, "If we had Christians who were half as committed as those people; we could take this country for God."

Commitment hasn't entirely gone out of style, but it has gone out of practice. It is high time we again learned that things which are worth having can only be purchased with the currency of commitment.

Think on This

1. In this selection I talked about the importance of commitment in reaching your goals in life. On a scale of one to ten, how does your commitment to your marriage rate?
2. Do you think Christians in general have less commitment than people of other religions? If yes, why?

3. Do you see the correlation between commitment and accomplishment, whether it is in marriage, business or politics?

Resource Reading
Joshua 1

The Marriage Saver of Commitment

"For this reason a man will leave his father and mother and be united to his wife, and they will become one flesh." (Genesis 2:24)

I f a disease were to afflict the majority of a populace," says veteran poll taker George Gallup, Jr., "spreading pain and dysfunction throughout all age groups, we would be frantically searching for reasons and solutions." Yet broken homes have become so common, contends Gallup, that the issue is not only neglected, it is ignored.[6]

What Gallup describes is not an isolated phenomenon but a worldwide scourge. In the former U.S.S.R. one marriage in three ends in divorce. In the United States one in two becomes a statistic. In China, the problem is swiftly growing to mirror the West. In the few Catholic countries such as the Philippines where church-related pressure has succeeded in disallowing divorce laws, broken homes still tear families apart and annulment has become the respected means of dissolving bad marriages.

In the past three decades the number of broken homes the world over has increased by a factor of 2.5.[7] We have finally come to realize that the mad quest for happiness and fulfillment usually ends in a bitter delusion which has devastating consequences for the generation of children who have grown up in single parent homes.

Women have learned through bitter experience that child support—to say nothing of emotional support—is usually sadly lacking when a marriage fails. Bone-weariness, excruciating loneliness, financial difficulty and emotional fatigue have challenged the idea that independence is the best thing. We have tragically learned what God taught us long ago: marriage is not for perfect people, but imperfect people who need each other. No matter how imperfect a husband or a wife may be, or how imperfect the institution of marriage may be, it is still the best way to meet human needs and pass on values to our children, generation after generation.

Commitment is an inner attitude, not an external form.

In recent days, walking away from a troubled marriage has lost some of its glamour and its boldness. As a twenty-eight-year-old newlywed put it, "My divorced mother wound up bitter and lonely. I'm going to do everything it takes to stay married for life."

When it's all said and done, nothing is more important to a marriage than the attitude which says, "No matter what our problems may be, we're committed to this marriage. Someway, somehow, we're going to find a solution!" Commitment is an inner attitude, not an external form. It is more than coming home to a mate, or refusing to let your eyes roam or your thoughts fantasize; it is the absolute refusal to even think of another person.

However, commitment is not meant to be a resignation. We are not to adopt the attitude of "Well, God doesn't want me to walk out on my mate so I guess I'm stuck with this marriage!" Commitment should be a positive force that doesn't even think of divorce as a problem solving technique. It recognizes that God has a better way, which in the long run can bring fulfillment and provide a stable environment in which your children can grow up. Commitment is the glue that keeps you from destroying

Insight

W*hen you honor the "till death us do part" commitment you made at the marriage altar, your focus goes beyond the irritation to the immediate anticipation that tomorrow will be better.*

what is threatened so that your marriage can mend and heal and be stronger than it ever was before.

Think on This

1. When you are confronted with a problem in your marriage, are you committed to working out the problem or are you tempted just to give up? Can you talk about problems openly?
2. Do you view commitment as a positive encouragement to problem solving, as opposed to utter resignation to a bad situation which you are afraid to disrupt?

Resource Reading
1 Corinthians 7:1-7

Part II

to have and to hold

Love Is a Decision, a Commitment to Care

"Love doesn't make the world go round;
it makes the ride worthwhile."[8]
—Franklin Adams

Love Makes
the Ride Worthwhile

*"If I speak in the tongues of men and of angels,
but have not love, I am only a resounding gong
or a clanging cymbal. . . . And now these three
remain: faith, hope and love. But the greatest of
these is love." (1 Corinthians 13:1, 13)*

I n Lewis Carroll's book *Alice's Adventures in Wonderland* there is a line which goes, "And the moral of that is 'Oh, tis love, tis love, that makes the world go round.' "[9] Franklin Adams disagrees, but he does believe that love is what makes the ride worthwhile. The reality, however, is that for many the ride is pretty tedious because theirs is a loveless relationship, a union of convenience or one which has grown stale and boring.

A marriage can exist without love. Thousands of men and women manage to stay married to each other and do not love each other. But it is a mechanical, wearisome, dull relationship far, far short of our expectation and God's provision. You can be happy without many things in life, but you can't be happily married without love.

Dr. David Olson, a marriage and family specialist from the University of Minnesota, believes that the vast majority of those who remain in a marriage without love are decidedly unhappy.

Before marriage, love is the deeply intoxicating, overwhelming conviction that you simply cannot live without someone. You literally swoon in the presence of that person. You worship the ground that he or she walks on. Yes—that's love. Or so we think. We send valentines, flowers and messages expressing the fact that we cannot live without the other person. There is romance, faith, optimism, exhilaration, acceptance, hope and sexual stimulation! This, we think, is love!

L*ove is a deep commitment, a decision to care, a binding decision to meet the needs of another person.*

Then you marry. How quickly things can change! I am thinking of a conversation which I heard as a husband told his wife that he felt she no longer loved him. With tears and angry, bitter words she replied, "How can you say that? I clean your house, raise your kids, do the washing and ironing, and you say I don't love you!"

What is love? I asked myself that question the day a young couple came for counseling. He had fathered a child by a young woman who had worked in his office. Yet I noticed that the large, silver belt buckle he wore bore the word, L-O-V-E. Too often love is really spelled L-U-S-T.

Love—the kind that keeps a marriage together, the same kind which Paul described in First Corinthians 13—is a deep commitment, a decision to care, a binding decision to meet the needs of another person.

We often think of love as the emotional infatuation of youth. But true, binding love bears the deep commitment of people who care for those who can no longer care for themselves. I am reminded of the deep commitment of Dr. Robertson C. McQuilkin, who cut short a meaningful career and resigned as President of Columbia International University to take care of his wife who had become afflicted with Alzheimer's disease. That signifies the real commitment of mature love.

Insight

Romantic love—the wild ecstasy of your first love—will be replaced by a deeper, more settled, abiding love which is like an anchor that allows the ship of your marriage to prevail no matter how the winds may blow.

Real love is not affected by the squalls of temptation, nor is it lessened by the ravages of time and aging when someone is no longer the person he was a few decades before.

Love, like a fire which has to be rekindled every morning, is kept alive through kind words, tender expressions of thoughtfulness and bottom-line acts such as carrying out the garbage and making the bed. It is important to express love but it is more important to demonstrate it.

Interested in saving your marriage? Read First Corinthians 13 with your mate, then ask God to let love be rekindled in your home and your heart.

Think on This

1. Life is like a journey in which there are peaks and valleys, yet it is the companionship you experience that

makes the journey worthwhile. Where are you in your relationship—a peak or a valley?

2. Love is usually considered an emotion (and that it is) but is that contradictory to the reality that love is a commitment, a decision to care no matter what your feelings may be?

3. If a marriage is loveless, is it hopeless?

Resource Reading
1 Corinthians 13:1-7

Getting the Message, "I Love You," Across

"How great is the love the Father has lavished on us, that we should be called children of God! And that is what we are! The reason the world does not know us is that it did not know him."
(1 John 3:1)

Some men find it difficult to say, "I love you." But in Bert Salva's case, what was tough was getting Mary Shiminsky—the object of his affection—to really believe him when he told her, "I love you." For almost four years Bert courted Mary but didn't get anywhere. Actually, what he got was a clear message of, "Get lost, buddy. I never want to see you again." To make the message more explicit, Mary changed her phone number, moved in with her parents who live in an isolated area and left no forwarding address.

Bert, however, didn't go away. He really loved her and wanted her to know that. Trying to find out where she was, Bert could only get a few leads. He knew the general area where she was but he didn't know her exact address. He thought and thought, and then he struck upon an idea.

There was one way, one slim chance by which he might convey the simple message, "I love you." He bought paint and a long-handled roller. He knew the way she went to work, and though he wasn't terribly confident it would work, he knew he had to try. In the darkness of the night he climbed on a three-story railroad trestle which spanned the highway near where Mary was living and painted a message. When she saw it, she knew who had painted it, but nobody else in the community knew.

T*he love of a husband or wife is important, but of far greater importance is the reality that God, whose love is constant and unfailing, will always love us no matter what we do, thereby giving us a pattern as to how we should love each other.*

Nobody had ever heard of Mary Shiminsky. But that desperate act—much like a quarterback's "hail Mary" thrown in the last three seconds of a football game—is what got her attention and eventually turned her heart. She saw the message, got in touch with Bert and a month later accepted his proposal of marriage. A year later twins arrived and blessed their home.

Four years later, with the mystery still unsolved in the community, Mary wrote to the newspaper admitting she was Mary Shiminsky and told the newspaper staff what had happened. Sensing a good story, they responded and sent out a reporter. Husband Bert told the reporter he didn't know if he could do it again—hanging three stories above the ground holding on to the railroad trestle with one hand and a paintbrush with the other—but he was convinced it was worth it. The message "I love you, Mary Shiminsky" got through.[10]

Do you ever marvel at the lengths to which someone like Bert will go to get a message across? Why is all of this so important? Psychiatrist William Glasser is convinced that only by giving and receiving love can one of the deepest of emotional needs be met. It is as necessary to normal human survival as is oxygen to the lungs and proper nutrition to the body.

Insight

Love is as necessary to human survival as is oxygen to the lungs and food to the body.

The cold reality, however, is that every woman doesn't have a Bert Salva who is willing to hang by one hand from a railroad trestle to get that message across. Some women desperately wish that the man they married would and could say those three words which make such a difference. But they never hear them.

Don't be like the old fellow whose wife asked, "Why don't you ever tell me that you love me? I think you do, but you never say it and it would mean so much to me." The old fellow cleared his throat and said, "Now, Sarah. If you will recall, before we got married I told you I loved you, and I also told you that if I ever changed my mind, I'd tell you that as well."

While hearing the words "I love you" may not be so important to men, they are vitally important to women. Saying, "I love you!"—even if you think she already knows it—reaffirms the deep commitment of your heart. It's important.

Even more important, however, is the fact that there is one who loves us unconditionally, who went to an amazing amount of trouble to get the message across. "For God so loved the world," wrote John "that he gave his one and only Son, that whoever believes in him shall not perish but have eternal life" (3:16). That's one incredible message of love.

The love of a husband or wife is important, but of far greater importance is the reality that God, whose love is constant and unfailing, will always love us no matter what we do, thereby giving us a pattern as to how we should love each other.

Think on This

1. How long has it been since you told your spouse that you love him or her? Daily? Once a week? When you want something in return? Make it a practice to reaffirm what he or she knows by expressing your love verbally and by so doing, keep the fire of love alive.
2. If you grew up in a culture where the verbal expression of love was not common or you are just uncomfortable with a verbal expression of love, try to *show* your love for your spouse each day. And although you don't *have* to verbalize it to demonstrate your love for someone, you may well choose to break with your past and discover how important and fulfilling it can be to make it a habit.

Resource Reading
1 John 3

Falling in and out of Love

"Love suffers long and is kind; love does not envy; love does not parade itself, is not puffed up." (1 Corinthians 13:4, NKJV)

What is love? Yes, everybody knows it's what makes the world go round and drives our hormones, but are passion and love really the same thing? And can you fall in love like you fall into a ditch or a swimming pool when you lose your balance? Is love merely an emotion that swings back and forth?

Psychologists tell us that romantic love—the kind that makes your head spin and your hormones rage—lasts on the average about two years beyond marriage, provided you have a marriage as opposed to what is now referred to as "a relationship."

C.S. Lewis, who, after being a confirmed bachelor for years, married and then learned the meaning of love, reflected on the vagaries of love in his book *Mere Christianity*. "Being in love," he wrote, "is a good thing, but it is not the best thing. There are many things below it, but there are also things above it. You cannot make it the basis of a whole life. It is a noble feeling but it is still a feeling. Now, no feeling can be relied on to last in its full intensity, or even to last at all. . . . In fact," he says, "the state of being in love does not last. . . . But of course ceasing to be 'in love' need not mean ceasing to love." Love, he contended, is what fuels the engine of marriage, but "being in love" was the explosion that started it.[11]

W*hat makes the business of cohabiting apart from the commitment of marriage so dangerous is that the whole business is based on the touchy-feely issues of emotion and eroticism.*

What makes the business of cohabiting apart from the commitment of marriage so dangerous is that the whole business is based on the touchy-feely issues of emotion and eroticism. Love, the authentic kind that keeps a man coming home to his wife and keeps the bond she has with him intact no matter what her emotions, is a commitment, a decision to be there, and it is the assurance that the other person will be there as well.

In many places in the world marriages are arranged and not the result of attraction. When I first encountered this I thought, *There is no way these marriages can work apart from romance!* But in due time, I learned that they not only endure, but in many situations they also prove to be far stronger than the average relationship where the mutual attraction was merely how beautiful or how handsome someone was.

Do they have problems? Certainly, just as those who fall in love have problems, but the difference is that in many arranged marriages, families are there to support, to encourage and to be a firewall against walking out on a mate. And, to my great surprise, in due time love often takes root and grows into a deep commitment to the one whom the bride or bridegroom hardly knew at the altar.

Insight

Like the roots of a tree which are unseen but hold the tree steady in a storm, love goes deep into the soil of life and holds marriages together when sickness, financial reversals and tragedies threaten to uproot us.

No, I'm not suggesting that this be the norm. But we should dispense with the thinking that it is normal to fall in and out of love with one person, then fall in love with another. Like the strong oak that has weathered the storm, the marriage which survives the winds of turmoil and the stress of life grows stronger with the passing of time.

It is time to disengage ourselves from the turbulence of living with emotions, with our senses saturated with feelings and to accept that love—the living, enduring kind—can be there no matter what the temperature of the heart may be.

That's the kind of love that endures.

Think on This

1. When tragedy strikes, marriages often fail. Why? Is love not strong enough to meet the need for stability?
2. On a personal level, what have you encountered that could have destroyed your marriage?

3. How does your faith in God help you through tough times?

Resource Reading
1 Corinthians 13:8-13

Rekindling the Fire of Love

"Then one of the seraphs flew to me with a live coal in his hand, which he had taken with tongs from the altar. With it he touched my mouth and said, 'See, this has touched your lips; your guilt is taken away and your sin atoned for.' "
(Isaiah 6:6-7)

T he afternoon was cold and crisp. My wife and I had stopped for the night in a colorful little German village fifty kilometers or so from the Frankfurt airport. As we often do after we get a room, we went for a walk to work the kinks out of our travel-weary legs.

I don't think I'll ever forget something I saw that evening because it so spoke to my heart. A young woman in her late twenties came down the stairs from a second-floor apartment carrying an empty coal shovel. We watched as she went to a home next door and then, a few minutes later, emerged with her shovel full of burning coals. She retraced her steps, carefully carrying the coals up the stairs so that none would spill. We stood there, curious. And then, in just a few moments, we noticed smoke curling from the top of the chimney in her apartment. The fire which had gone out was lit, and the coldness of an empty home gradually gave way to the warmth of a new fire.

As Darlene and I walked away hand in hand I couldn't help thinking of how many homes are like that—not cold because a fire has gone out in the furnace—but cold because the romance of first love has died.

All the counseling in the world will fall on deaf ears until you realize that God alone changes the hearts of people, and that only He can rekindle the fires of love which at one time warmed your hearts and lives.

In over three decades of counseling and working with people, I've lost track of the number of times I've heard the words: "I used to love her, but I don't know if I love her anymore" or "I don't think I can love him after what he's done to me." The fire's gone out. But the questions are: Can it be rekindled? Can we go to the hearth of God's altar and say, "Lord, the fire's gone out of our marriage. Our hearts are cold. We feel like quitting, but we believe You can help us"?

All the counseling in the world will fall on deaf ears until you realize that God alone changes the hearts of people, and that only He can rekindle the fires of love which at one time warmed your hearts and lives. I am convinced that one of the greatest mistakes people make is giving up on a marriage because they are looking for help in the wrong place.

Marriage involves a spiritual relationship. You and your mate became one—emotionally, physically and, perhaps, at one time even spiritually. Seeking God's help includes a spiritual dimension as you humbly realize your sin and failure and seek forgiveness and restoration. When you take that step you allow the Holy Spirit to begin to rekindle the fire within.

Insight

*W*hen your heart is right with God and you ask for His help, there is a synergism at work—God's Holy Spirit does what you cannot do (especially in the heart of another), and your attitude changes, making you more caring and more loving.*

Love is very much like a fire which burns low in the cold night and must be fanned into flames again in the morning. Acts of kindness, gestures of thoughtfulness and even times when you keep your mouth shut when you would rather point out how bungling or careless your mate is all contribute to renewing the fires of love.

"But how can I be sure that the one who hurt me will not let me down?" people ask. That is a valid question, but the answer certifies the obvious. There is always risk to love, but apart from taking that risk there is no hope that things can ever be different.

If your marriage has failed, you have every reason to be disappointed, but consider the other side of the ledger. Rebuilding what failure has threatened always comes with the blessing of God.

How about it? Have I described the need of your life? Then take the hand of your spouse, bow your heads and pray, "Lord, rekindle the fire, and start the work in me, today." You'll be amazed at what happens. Of that I am certain.

Think on This

1. Before you lay down an ultimatum—"You do this or else"—think through the consequences. Is this really what you want? Ask another question: Is this what God wants?
2. What are the alternatives? If there are none, can you wait patiently for the Lord to do what only He can bring about? If your answer is no, why not?
3. Ask your mate to pray with you about what you can do to be more loving, caring and sensitive.

Resource Reading
Colossians 3:12-19

Falling in
Love Twice

"Husbands, love your wives, just as Christ loved the church and gave himself up for her." (Ephesians 5:25)

C an you fall in love twice? "Absolutely!" Kim and Krickitt Carpenter would tell you. They know! In a recently published book entitled *The Vow*, they tell their story.[12]

On the night of November 24, 1993, newlyweds Kim and Krickitt were on their way to visit her parents when they were involved in a terrible automobile accident that almost killed them both. Krickitt was in a coma for two weeks, and when she wakened from the dark night, she had no short-term memory. When she was able to talk to Kim, who had recovered more quickly than she, she looked at him and said, "I don't know you; I don't want you; go back to where you came from." She kept talking about Todd, her boyfriend of some four years before.

She knew her parents and clearly remembered things that had happened years previous; but she did not know her husband, and much worse than that, she certainly did not love him. Kim was crushed, and felt as though he was married to the living dead. Statistics say that eighty to ninety percent of those who sustain brain damage end up divorcing their spouse because their personalities have been radically altered and they have become like strangers, sometimes hostile ones at that.

So why didn't Kim give up on Krickitt? When asked that question, Kim answered, "When you make a vow before the Lord, you need to be a person of your word." Both Kim and Krickitt were committed Christians and had taken their marriage vows seriously when they stood at the marriage altar and pledged "till death us do part."

L*ove is more than an emotion;
it is a deep, meaningful commitment.*

Kim stood by Krickitt, helped her in rehabilitation, brought flowers to her and did many other small things to express his love for her. The storybook ending to this near tragedy is that eventually Krickitt, wearing the same wedding dress that she had worn when she first took her vows, had another ceremony—just like the first one—where she and Kim reaffirmed their love and commitment to each other. Love was born a second time in her heart.

Question: Can you learn to love someone a second time? When someone you love has trampled on his or her vows and in a moment of thoughtless passion, violated the commitment he or she made, can love be reborn?

I'm thinking of a couple who sat with me only a few days ago. The husband began by saying, "There's nothing that you can do to help us. We've been to many counselors and I don't think that there is any hope for our marriage." I turned to them and said, "I'm so sorry to hear that God has died, and with His death any hope of His doing anything in your lives also expired!"

They looked at me as if I was crazy. "Look," I said, "as long as God and both of you are alive, there is hope that your love for each other can be rekindled."

Kim courted his wife just as he did the first time. They got to know each other, and they talked about the Lord and what God had meant to each of them. Eventually, she learned to trust him, to love him and to recommit herself to him. The process is the same whether it is a fiery automobile crash that wipes out your short-term memory or a devastating

Insight

Though the circumstances of your life are different, what God did for Kim and Krickitt Carpenter He can do for you, because anything is possible with God.

moral failure that destroys your long-term memories. The way back is the same.

Love is more than an emotion; it is a deep, meaningful commitment, and rediscovering that has made Kim and Krickitt Carpenter's marriage a twofold blessing which has endured the fire and will endure the test of time.

Think on This

1. Do people give up too quickly on relationships? Have you done that? Are you considering calling it quits right now?

2. When asked why he didn't just give up on the situation, Kim replied that when you make a vow before God, you need to keep it. Do you agree?

Resource Reading
Hosea 1:1-10; 3:1-5

Love Spoken Here

"And now these three remain: faith, hope and love. But the greatest of these is love." (1 Corinthians 13:13)

When I walked to the door of a neighbor for the first time I was surprised to see a freshly painted sign on the door. No, not a quarantine sign warning of an infectious disease, but it did generate almost as much surprise. The notice read simply, "LOVE SPOKEN HERE." Word had circulated in the neighborhood that this family had become Christians, and as a positive sign the back window of the old van that once had been painted with psychedelic colors now bore the message, "Let the Son shine in." I could not help wondering what was behind all of this.

As I got acquainted with the young couple who lived there, I learned in short order that love had not always been the language that had been spoken in that home. In fact, that couple's marriage had been on the rocks—driven there by alcohol, drugs and flaring tempers—when a friend invited them to attend an informal Bible study in a neighbor's home. They had tried just about everything from psychology to Eastern religions, so they figured, "Why not try out one more religion? What harm can it do?"

Skeptical at first, they began to discover that the language of the Bible is really the language of love. It is the language of God's love for people who find it easier to hate than to love. Over a period of time the couple met Jesus Christ, the chief actor in the story of redemption. When they invited Him into their lives, their lives and home were changed. They learned a new language—the language of love. They also discovered that what Paul wrote to the Corinthians was true, that "if anyone is in Christ, he is a new creation; the old has gone, the new has come!" (2 Corinthians 5:17).

I *am fully convinced that the real kind of love, the kind that replaces selfishness and greed, comes only as the God of love takes up residence in our hearts and homes.*

It seems that in recent years so many things have changed in our world, yet at the same time it seems nothing has really changed. What does that mean? In spite of technology and instant communication, it seems we're still not connecting with each other. The same old problems which seem to tear us apart are the very ones that writers of Scripture talked about when the Bible was being written.

The good news, however, is that the remedy to the problems of the first century are still the answer to our needs in the twenty-first century. Hatred and indifference give way to service and care born of love. John wrote, "Whoever does not love does not know God, because God is love" (1 John 4:8). To a society which didn't know the difference between lust and love, Paul wrote, "The love of God is shed abroad in our hearts by the Holy Ghost which is given unto us" (Romans 5:5, KJV).

By the way, what language do you speak in your home? No, I don't mean English, Tagalog, Spanish or Mandarin. Put another way, is it the language of selfishness and anger or the magnificent language called LOVE? I am fully convinced that the real kind of love, the kind that

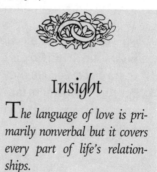

Insight

The language of love is primarily nonverbal but it covers every part of life's relationships.

replaces selfishness and greed, comes only as the God of love takes up residence in our hearts and homes.

It is little wonder that the language of love is so seldom spoken in our homes and lives. Until we know the God of love and He becomes our Father, there is little likelihood that we will speak His language. You can't be His child and learn His language until you are adopted into His family and embrace Him as your Father.

How did you answer the question about what language you speak in your home? If you are not sure, why not plant a tape recorder somewhere and, without your family members knowing, record the conversation that takes place around your dinner table. If you don't like what you hear, then learn that language which speaks heart to heart—the language of love. It's the one taught by the Father to His children whose lives have been changed by His Spirit.

Think on This

1. Do you feel that it is acceptable to say things to members of your family—the plain, unvarnished truth—when you would never say the same thing to a stranger? Why?
2. Do you see a connection between the statement in First John 4:16 (God is love) and the fact that we learn to love because He indwells our lives?
3. For further insights into the relationship between love and our lives see Romans 5:5, Galatians 5:22-23 and John 3:16.

Resource Reading
John 11

Part III

Getting What You Expect

"A deaf husband and a blind wife are a happy couple."

—Danish proverb

Wben Is
Enougb Enougb?

*" 'It was because your hearts were hard that
Moses wrote you this law.' '. . . Therefore what
God has joined together, let man not sepa-
rate.' " (Mark 10:5, 9)*

Strange things happen in Israel. I'm not sure if it is
the climate, the culture, the water or the air that
makes people so stubborn. Take, for example, the battle
that Yahiya Avraham fought. First he fought with his
wife, Ora. Then with the rabbis. Then with the court system. You see, the Avrahams were married in Yemen
when she was twelve and he was twenty-eight. There
wasn't a lot of romance in their relationship, but that's
how they did things a few decades ago. Ora, the wife, told
an Israeli newspaper that the problems started when she
bore her husband two daughters. He wanted sons.

Twelve years into the marriage she had had enough and
left him. By then they were living in Israel, where the issue
of marriage and divorce is left up to the rabbinate. She
wanted a divorce; Yahiya didn't. And what happened? In Israel, according to Jewish law, both parties must agree to a

divorce, and Mr. Avraham—being of the old school—said, "No!"

The rabbis tried reason. It didn't work. They tried to bribe him, offering him a fancy apartment. They promised religious blessings. One of the rabbis even sang melancholy songs in Yemeni, Mr. Avraham's native tongue, to soften his heart—that didn't work either.

Then, they tried more stern measures. Israeli law allows the rabbis, as a last resort, to send a man to prison so that he may have time to think through domestic issues. So the good rabbis in Jerusalem sent Mr. Avraham to jail.

And, sadly, that's where he spent thirty years of his life. He holds the record for being in prison simply because he wouldn't give his wife a divorce. Age and prison time did not soften Mr. Avraham's resolve. When given a chance to change his mind he was quoted as saying, "Can't do it, can't do it, go away."

W*hen two people—no matter how flawed and human—are committed to saving a marriage, it can be done. It's a proven fact.*

And what does his wife say? "He destroyed my life, may his name be destroyed. I haven't seen his ugly puss since 1967 and I hope never to see him again." Tough stuff those Avrahams!

Mr. Avraham recently died there in Ayalon Prison in Tel Aviv, still married to Ora, who did not mourn his passing. Today we shake our heads in disbelief—both at the system and at his stubbornness. Yet there is something about this eighty-year-old man's tenacity that I can't help but admire. His stubbornness and refusal to concede to a divorce are admirable because divorce is a thing we should avoid if at all possible. But admittedly his energies could have been better spent in trying to fix his marriage rather than wasting his time in jail.

Mr. Avraham went about trying to keep his marriage alive in completely the wrong way, but I've worked with people long enough to know for a fact that scores of relationships could be salvaged if some tenacity and stubbornness were applied. I'm not suggesting that we lock up one of the marriage partners until he

Insight

God doesn't want us to "strain at a gnat and swallow a camel" and thereby be perhaps legally right but practically wrong.

or she comes to their senses, but I would suggest that taking a little time to consider the consequences of breaking up a marriage could do a world of good.

But instead of taking time to try and work things out, at the first sign of distress people often think that changing partners is the only answer. They give up too soon. Dissolving relationships doesn't dissolve problems. They are merely carried into future relationships. People, with God's help, solve problems. Court systems or jails never change hearts. Only God does that.

I'm thinking of a letter written by a listener to *Guidelines*. A young woman told how she had divorced her husband of twelve years because she didn't like some of his habits. Then she wrote, "Now I have become a Christian, and I know what I did was wrong." Then wistfully, she added, "If I had only known how to pray."

Before you give up on your marriage, sit down and count the cost. Prayerfully say, "God, is there no way to find a solution to our lives? Show us Your will!" When two people—no matter how flawed and human—are committed to saving a marriage, it can be done. It's a proven fact.

Think on This

1. Do you think that some people give up too quickly on relationships?
2. This week focus on saying or doing something nice to or for your mate. Make a sincere attempt to express your appreciation to him or her.
3. When two people—no matter how different they may be—are both committed to God's will for their lives, He will show them what to do. How far are you willing to bend? When disagreements arise, ask yourself, "How important is this, anyway? What will it matter this time next week—perhaps even this time tomorrow?"

Resource Reading
Mark 10:1-10

Overcoming Your Tendency to "Lose It"

*"Bear with each other and forgive whatever griev-
ances you may have against one another. Forgive
as the Lord forgave you." (Colossians 3:13)*

W hat happened to your forehead?" I asked a
young woman who had come for counseling.
"Oh—that!" she said. "I bumped into the door." It didn't
take long for the truth to come out. It was her husband's
fist that she had run into—not the door.

"How could this have happened?" I have asked myself
more than once. Though I never have said it, I have felt like
telling some men: "Look, this is the woman who stood by
your side at the marriage altar, the one whom you promised to love and to cherish until death separated you. You
told me that you couldn't live without her, but now it
seems that you can't live with her. What went wrong?"

Possibly such bluntness would be justified, but it
wouldn't necessarily be all that helpful. I *can* tell you with
relative certainty what went wrong. First, each spouse began to take the other for granted. With marriage there
sometimes comes a familiarity which seems to allow for

open season with each other. Husbands and wives begin to talk to each other in ways that would never be tolerated in a work or social environment.

Then comes escalating tension and difficulty. Annoyances are catalogued but not diffused. Stress tends to cause each to blame the other for problems. At times people who really do love each other have so little discipline in their personal lives that they call each other names— derogatory terms which are intended to demean and hurt. For instance, one husband complained bitterly to his wife, "You make me so mad I could just bite your head off." She just smiled and replied, "Why, dear, if you did that you'd have more brains in your stomach than you do in your head."

There is never a place for sarcasm or verbal abuse in a relationship. Such verbal license allows both husbands and wives to say and do things which they may live to regret deeply.

> *Changed hearts result in changed lives, and changed lives are what the good news of the gospel is all about.*

Verbal abuse *always* precedes physical abuse, and physical abuse tends to repeat itself from generation to generation. The child who grows up in a family where there is abuse is apt to deeply resent it in the marriage of his or her parents, but may eventually become abusive himself or herself, having never learned how to properly resolve conflict or diffuse disagreements.

"Look, I'll never hit you again as long as I live. I promise! Besides it was your fault, too!" That is not the way to stop the cycle of abuse. So, how is a deadly situation forever diffused?

First, call violence what it is—sin! Never, ever is there justification for abuse, either physical or verbal. God says it is wrong (period), and for you to trivialize the wrongdoing only opens the door for repeated and more violent failures.

The second step is to make yourself accountable to someone outside your family. Rarely is there ever a situation in which only one act of violence occurs, but every battered individual was, at one time, a victim *for the first time*. At the first occurrence, someone else needs to know: a par-

Insight

The temptation to bully another person—especially your spouse—is a reflection of deep insecurity. It never works!

ent, a pastor, a counselor, perhaps even the authorities. Violence must be countered with strong love, the kind that says and means, "If there is ever a second occurrence, I'm out of here—permanently—until you have had counseling and can demonstrate that you have your temper and your tongue under control."

The third very important step is discipline, both personal and spiritual. Knowing that verbal abuse or violence is intolerable prods us to find ways to handle dissatisfaction and deal with stress. Prayer, exercise, counseling and discipline are all part of our resources in helping us to be loving and kind. Changed hearts result in changed lives, and changed lives are what the good news of the gospel is all about.

Think on This

1. If you were a victim of violence growing up, no matter how deeply you resented it, you are more prone to reproduce that same behavior. If you feel that you are capable of "losing it," get help before you do.
2. Saying "it was your fault as much as it was mine" is a failure to take responsibility for your actions. Far better is saying, "What I said was wrong and I want your forgiveness." Then replay the situation in your thinking. At what point did you fall back on "bullying tactics" as opposed to expressing your thoughts?
3. If someone has been abusive with you, there need to be ground rules for a continued relationship, with a third party fully cognizant of the situation. Submitting to that discipline is part of the healing process and it also allows the other person to renew the relationship.

Resource Reading
Colossians 3:1-17

I'm the Boss!
...Oh, Yeah?

*"Wives, submit to your husbands as to the Lord.
For the husband is the head of the wife as Christ
is the head of the church." (Ephesians 5:22-23)*

W hen Southern Baptists adopted a position paper stating that wives are to "submit graciously" to their husbands, it created far more controversy than if Paul had inadvertently taken a ham sandwich into a synagogue. Relationships between husbands and wives began disintegrating into shouting matches, so the denomination reasserted what Paul wrote to the Ephesians: that God has established an order when it comes to leadership in the family and that wives are to submit to their husbands as unto the Lord (see Ephesians 5:22-24).

When I heard of the controversy that arose from that issue I wasn't surprised that the world didn't get it. The secular press jumped on the issue, blowing it all out of proportion, depicting husbands as dictators who wanted their women barefoot and pregnant, cooking big meals in the kitchen—a combination of domestic servant and sex-slave. The world never accepts biblical principles and we can't expect it to understand them. Writing to the Corinthians, Paul said that the natural or unregenerated person doesn't understand the things of the Spirit of God (see 1 Corinthians 2:14).

But what did surprise me was the way some in the household of faith scoffed at the issue. On a talk show one well-known Christian television personality said that the passage in Ephesians is "not an important one" and further undermined what Paul said by saying that since Paul was not married (at least in his opinion), he didn't know what he was talking about anyway. I think Martin Luther would have taken strong exception with that position as would have Charles Wesley, Dwight L. Moody and scores of others.

A seminary professor once said that text without context is pretext, and that's where this whole issue goes astray. Paul, who incidentally would have refuted the position that it's up to the reader to decide what's important and what's not, went on record saying that "all scripture is given by inspiration of God" (2 Timothy 3:16, KJV).

T*he world never accepts biblical principles and we can't expect it to understand them.*

Why so much confusion as to what God's order is? The word which Paul used for submission is a Greek word which is a combination of two words: *hupo*, a preposition meaning under, and *tasso*, a verb which means to stand. Hence, when someone was in subjection, he stood under the authority of one to whom greater authority had been given. It had nothing whatsoever to do with inequalities of any kind. It never meant one was better than the other, had more intelligence than the other or knew more about leadership. But it did mean every soldier had differing responsibilities and each was accountable to someone higher in rank.

Immediately before the directive to women, Paul stresses the fact that both husbands and wives are to be submissive to each other, and he uses the same word which he later directs specifically to wives. When husbands and wives are

Insight

W_{hile} *God places the responsibility for leadership on the shoulders of a husband, there is no conflict with recognizing that a wife is his equal and that God wants both to be respectful and cooperative with each other.*

quick to defer to the other, to be sensitive to each other's needs and to strive to meet them, they are doing exactly what Paul ordered.

The specific direction to women is his way of saying, "Men I want you to lead the way. I hold you responsible for the welfare of your wife and children. So women, let them lead." Zig Zigler says, "Even a two-car parade gets fouled up if you don't decide ahead of time who's going to lead."[13]

Speaking of leadership, I'm reminded of the comment of Margaret Thatcher, who said that when someone has to stand up and say, "I'm the leader," he's not the leader. If someone holds a gun on you, it's amazing how cooperative and submissive you become, but when you really love someone and know he loves you the same way, it's easy to defer to that person and let him lead the way. That's the point Paul was really striving to get across.

Think on This

1. If a spaceship landed in your front yard and a little green man with antennae knocked on your door and asked, "Who's in charge here?" what would your youngster say if he answered the door?
2. Do you agree that should a husband have to say, "I'm the leader," he's either very insecure or else he's not the leader?
3. Leadership styles vary from dictators on one extreme to a democratic consensus on the other extreme. What style of leadership is present in your home? Who's the leader? Or would you say, "We both are!" Or, "Actually, our kids call the shots here!"?

Resource Reading
Ephesians 5:15-33

I'm Sitting Down Outside but Standing Up Inside[14]

"Husbands, love your wives, just as Christ loved the church and gave himself up for her." (Ephesians 5:25)

I have been involved in ministry to families for more than four decades, and I have come to the conclusion that one of the most confusing and easily misunderstood biblical concepts is how God wants husbands and wives to relate to each other. In Christian circles, most men remember Paul's directive to women that they are to be submissive—ah yes, how could they forget? And women are quick to remember that husbands are to love their wives as Christ loved the church—something which many men are grossly negligent in doing. Amazing, isn't it, that we always remember what the other is supposed to do while we forget what we ourselves are supposed to do?

The popular conception is that women are supposed to knuckle under to their husbands, who treat them as domestic inferiors. Women are supposed to take it and smile, not upsetting the fragile egos of their men, never forgetting that it was Eve who took the fruit.

That may be the accepted script, but it isn't the biblical one. In many cultures of the world, women are treated as inferiors and are often reduced to the level of servitude. Though it is legal in Papua, New Guinea and illegal in India, in both countries bride prices are paid to a woman's family, reducing women to the level of chattel, making them not much better than livestock.

Recently an article appeared in papers which read as follows: "Afghanistan's Taliban religious army abruptly ordered the closure Tuesday of more than 100 private schools that have been educating girls in defiance of bans aimed at keeping women and girls at home."[15] Think for a moment of the impact of what I just quoted—no education apart from religious instruction in the Koran for girls under eight and no future in a modern world.

It is high time we returned to the timeless
principles found in God's Word, for only then
will the war between the sexes come to a halt.

The May 16, 1998 issue of the *Bangalore Times* in India says that "neither law nor propaganda has helped in bringing down the number of girls falling prey to dowry menace every year." The article explains that between 1987 and 1994, an average of 5,000 girls every year met their deaths because husbands dissatisfied with their wives could not get a refund of their dowry and took out their hostilities on the girls they had married.

Many cultures and religions strive to repress women, but Christianity has sought to elevate them. It is for this reason that women in the West are generally treated as equals, not as inferiors—an outgrowth of the influence of Christianity in law and culture.

Paul directs that men are to love their wives as Christ loved the church—not to treat them as chattel or to repress them and keep them ignorant, allowing them only to learn to cook, clean and sew or do menial labor. Both husbands and wives are to submit to each other, while wives are to allow husbands to lead the family.

The truth of the matter is that the farther we move from the biblical model and pattern—whether it is the extremes which I referred to earlier or the actions of repressive husbands who think they have the right to be dictators—the more out of kilter society is going to be. It is high time we returned to the timeless principles found in God's Word, for only then will the war between the sexes come to a halt and will we begin to find the happiness and harmony which God, the Creator and Architect of the family, designed for His children.

Insight

N*o other religion in all the world has elevated the place of women as has Christianity, but, in reality, becoming a Christian is not embracing a religion but entering a relationship with the person of Jesus Christ.*

Think on this

1. Attitude is everything. When one says, "I'm the head of this house!" as a dictator, he is just as wrong as if he were to add, "And I have my wife's permission to say so!" How is a partnership whereby a husband provides leadership different than a dictatorship?

2. What parallels do you see between God's plan for marriage and five men on a basketball court?

Resource Reading
Titus 2:1-8

I Love You, You're Perfect ... Now Change[16]

"I ask you to receive her in the Lord in a way worthy of the saints and to give her any help she may need from you, for she has been a great help to many people, including me." (Romans 16:2)

I Love You, You're Perfect ... Now Change is the name of a humorous play which is a kind of parody on how people often fall madly in love with someone, think the person is just wonderful and then strive to remake him or her. Sometimes they nag. Sometimes they cajole, sometimes they manipulate, sometimes they threaten. But it just doesn't work. It's a lot like teaching a pig to sing: it annoys the pig and it wastes your time. Yet from the days of Adam and Eve to the present, people have striven to redo the person to whom they are married.

I love you, you're perfect ... now change. That was the mentality of a Yemenite Jew who moved to Israel. As you probably know, Yemen is a very primitive country, and when Abe and Sarah arrived in Tel Aviv, they were absolutely agog at the modern conveniences and things which they had never before seen.

One day Abe wandered into a high rise in Tel Aviv and saw an old woman, her hair covered with a babushka, her face a maze of wrinkles, with one gnarled hand firmly gripping a cane make her way into an elevator. Abe stood there spellbound. Never before had he seen an elevator. In moments the doors of the elevator opened again and out walked a beautiful young woman—at least forty years younger than the woman who had walked through the sliding doors moments before.

Abe stroked his beard, and with a sly smile did a half-moon between his whiskers. Poking his finger toward the elevator he said, "I think I will send Sarah into that thing!"

I love you, you're perfect . . . now change.

I *love you. You're perfect. Now let's grow together and change as God works in our lives. That's the better way.*

In all fairness, it isn't only men who want change. It works on both sides of the gender issue. I often tell young women that there are three words which are on the minds of brides when they marry. One word is aisle—the aisle down which she will walk on her father's arm. Another is the word altar—where she will kneel. And the third is the word hymn. You know—the hymn which will be sung during the ceremony. And, I suggest, those same words are there after the ceremony as well, "I'll alter him," but after the ceremony they're spelled a little differently.

I love you, you're perfect . . . now change. OK, bottom line. In all honesty, do you find yourself trying to change your spouse? If you really want change, try these simple guidelines which are guaranteed to work.

Guideline #1: Stop trying to get your mate to change and love him "as is." Love begins where a person is. Understand that change is the result of God's Holy Spirit working in a person's life. There has to be a motive for change, and your being on someone's case isn't sufficient to affect long-term changes.

Insight

Loving someone as he or she is, with the expectancy that God can make the person into what He wants, is the surest path to what you really would like to see take place.

Guideline #2: Strive to be the person God wants *you* to be. We often spend so much time and energy trying to get our spouse to change that we don't take the time to concentrate on being the person we ought to be. Focus on being the right person, not on making the other person right.

Guideline #3: Start praying that God will do His work in the other person's heart. We can only try to change someone from the outside. We can't get inside the heart, but God can.

I love you, you're perfect . . . now change. It just doesn't work. But the good news is that we can and do change. As we conform to what God wants, we understand how much we do love the other person, and then strive to please the one whom we love. I love you. You're perfect. Now let's grow together and change as God works in our lives. That's the better way.

Think on This

1. Concentrate on being the right person, not on making the other person right.

2. One woman said, "I thought I was marrying 'Mr. Right,' but after we got married, he turned into 'Mr. Always Right.'" What happened? Do you think she really knew the man she married? Had he fooled her into thinking he was something else than he really was, or was she simply blind, hoping that he would turn into something else?

Resource Reading
Ephesians 5

Part IV

Infidelity and Your Marriage

"Marriage used to be a contract. Now many regard it as a ninety-day option."[17]

—James Hewett

The Dark Side of Human Nature[18]

"Cleanse me with hyssop, and I will be clean;
*   wash me, and I will be whiter than snow.*
Let me hear joy and gladness;
*   let the bones you have crushed rejoice.*
Hide your face from my sins
*   and blot out all my iniquity.*
Create in me a pure heart, O God,
*   and renew a steadfast spirit within me."*
(Psalm 51:7-10)

Infidelity. Marriage counselors agree that it rears its ugly head in the majority of broken homes. Filmmakers and TV producers may make it look natural, romantic and free, but its consequences are devastating beyond description.

The proliferation of sex in the media today has gone far, far beyond that which ever could have been imagined a generation ago. Today you can't watch an evening of television without being exposed to explicit sexuality. One observer contends that for every media depiction of a husband and wife loving each other there are at least fifteen encounters of two individuals engaged in sex who are not married to each other.

Fidelity to the one who stood by your side at the marriage altar is considered passé. But what the media doesn't show is the guilt, heartache, loneliness and emptiness of a life which has been plowed under by infidelity. This, of course, doesn't fill seats in a theater or demand prime time exposure.

No relationship in all the world can be compared to that of two people who love each other, after having gone public with their commitment in marriage, giving themselves to each other sexually. This relationship is not only blessed by God Himself but involves the emotional, the physical and the spiritual aspects of human life. "Undefiled and pure" are the Greek words used in Hebrews 13:4 to describe it. The Old Testament allegory, the Song of Solomon, uses the relationship of a husband and wife to depict God's love for Israel, and some say it is also a picture of Christ's love for His body, the Church.

---

*I*nfidelity is hell, and its consequences
of anguish and pain reach beyond the
darkness of a sleepless night.

The cheapening of marriage and the trivialization of the relationship between husband and wife has reduced sexuality to the level of animal lust which should be satisfied at the slightest suggestion of opportunity.

In the 1960s morality began to change. For a period of time sexual license was applauded as being free and beautiful. Then, people began to realize that there is a bonding in marriage which cannot be broken apart from anger, hostility and jealousy. Sharing your husband or wife with someone else is not something that can be done without tremendous emotional upheaval. In more cases than not, it results in rejection and divorce.

Insight

While few think much about it, there is an emotional bonding when sexual intercourse takes place which denies that sex is casual or recreational.

What the media doesn't tell you is what David learned long ago: Infidelity is hell, and its consequences of anguish and pain reach beyond the darkness of a sleepless night. Take time to read Psalm 51, where David cries out to God asking for forgiveness and restoration.

"I thought I was doing what I wanted to do," writes one friend of *Guidelines*, explaining why she became involved with another man, "but now I realize that I was destroying the very thing I really wanted." What the media doesn't tell you about infidelity, you may learn the hard way.

Think on This

1. Why do women in particular find it difficult to say "Good-bye" when there has been a sexual encounter?
2. Do you think our generation has begun to realize that the openness of sexual expression during the last several decades had consequences that few (especially men) considered?
3. Is there such a thing as "safe sex" for anybody, but especially for those who live with the realization that God has placed boundaries for those who belong to Him?

4. This section focuses on the consequences of infidelity as well as the way back from infidelity. Though this may not particularly apply to you, the biblical principles discussed in this section will help strengthen your relationship and equip you to help others.

Resource Reading
Psalm 51

The Price
of Infidelity

"Jealousy arouses a husband's fury, and he will show no mercy when he takes revenge." (Proverbs 6:34)

I nfidelity is not new, but in recent years we have begun treating it more casually than in any previous generation. The reality, however, is that its consequences are not lessened by a more liberal outlook on life. In most cases, infidelity is the crowning blow to marriages that may have already been on the rocks.

A survey done by *Bottom Line* magazine suggests that up to six out of ten women are unfaithful to their husbands.[19] But even more husbands are guilty. *Psychology Today* says, "More people say they have cheated on their marriage partners than on their tax returns or expense accounts."[20]

Why is infidelity so devastating to marriages? Why can't people just forgive their adulterous spouses and forget the hurt and pain infidelity has caused? The answer, simply put, is that human beings are not psychologically composed in such a way that an emotional switch can be thrown and everything clears the screen of memory and feelings. Jealousy, resentment, feelings of betrayal and breach of trust all make it difficult to just move on in life. Long ago the writer of Proverbs observed that "jealousy arouses a husband's fury, and he will show no mercy when he takes revenge" (Proverbs 6:34).

Don't buy into the myth that affairs can actually make your marriage stronger.

When the birth control pill was invented, thus separating sex from procreation for millions of people, a cultural revolution began which lowered the bar and loosened the restraints which had governed societal views of sexuality for centuries. Many people began taking advantage of this looser lifestyle, indulging in a sexual licentiousness which would previously have been unacceptable. But despite this change in society's view of sexual relationships, when men and women who consider themselves to be liberated and free from traditional restraints realize that their spouse is in someone else's arms, jealousy and resentment rage just as they did centuries ago, and marriages become casualties of this misaligned sophistry.

Why did God place a premium on fidelity in marriage? Because He made us and knew that our deep emotional needs could be met best through monogamous marriage. Remember, God's plan was, "For this reason a man will leave his father and mother and be united to his wife, and they will become one flesh" (Genesis 2:24), a formula which was endorsed by Jesus Himself.

But wait: if monogamy is part of God's plan, how did Solomon's 300 wives and 700 concubines and David's several wives fit in? A study of Scripture shows that from

Abraham's time to the Babylonian captivity, pagan practices involving polygamy influenced God's people but were never part of God's plan or purpose.

From the Babylonian captivity in 586 B.C. on through the entire New Testament, there are no statements or examples which would justify either polygamy or infidelity. To the contrary, leaders in the

Insight

While there is infidelity today and has been from the beginning of recorded history, God made us in such a way that we should disdain the very thought of sharing a husband or wife with another person.

church were to be husbands of one wife, and the context means, "married to just one person."

"But it's just the way men are made," I have been told by those choosing to justify their infidelity. Before you buy into that mentality, just listen to the feeble rationalizations of men who have voiced that logic and come out losers. You'll realize that it just doesn't work.

If there were no God, no Ten Commandments with the injunction, "You shall not commit adultery" (Exodus 20:14), no heaven or hell and no accountability to God, you would still discover that if you want a marriage to work, you had better be faithful to the one to whom you committed yourself.

Nothing less than that really works. Don't buy into the myth that affairs can actually make your marriage stronger. That's like believing that gargling with hydrochloric acid will take away your sore throat, or shooting yourself in the foot with a .45 is the best way to deal with an itch on your toe.

The author of Proverbs put it well when he said, "Can a man scoop fire into his lap without his clothes being burned? Can a man walk on hot coals without his feet being scorched? So is he who sleeps with another man's wife; no one who touches her will go unpunished" (6:27-29).

It's still true.

Think on This

1. While infidelity may be accepted somewhat more casually today than it was a generation ago, its consequences (usually fatal to a marriage) remain about the same. Why is this?
2. At times a husband or wife casually leaves "evidence" where the other person in the marriage can become aware of an affair. Why?
3. If you knew that your best friend was cheating on her husband—a friend of yours as well—would you feel "honor bound" to tell him? Or would you cover for the wife?

Resource Reading
Proverbs 6

The Steps to Adultery

"After the time of mourning was over, David had
her brought to his house, and she became his wife
and bore him a son. But the thing David had done
displeased the LORD." (2 Samuel 11:27)

Paul tells us in the New Testament that David was a man after God's own heart (Acts 13:22), something that was said of no other person whose life is chronicled in the Bible. He was the one who went up against the giant Goliath, the one who united the kingdom of Israel and defeated its enemies. Yet, tragically, it is for his affair with Bathsheba that history has most remembered David.

The world judges its own people by their greatest accomplishments, but it judges God's people by their greatest moral failures. The media never cared that Jimmy Swaggart had a ministry in South America to orphans, feeding thousands, housing and clothing street urchins, but he made front-page news for his sordid relationship with a prostitute. Neither did it care that Jim Bakker once touched the lives of millions for good and God, but it did make much of his moral and financial failures.

How do we explain what happened to David? A clue is found in the opening sentences of the sad story of David and Bathsheba. Samuel the prophet wrote, "In the spring, at the time when kings go off to war, David sent Joab out with the King's men . . ." (2 Samuel 11:1). He was in the *wrong* place at the *wrong* time, the same failure which has accounted for many a person's eventual infidelity.

Digressing for a moment, you may remember that when Joshua and the army met defeat at the conquest of Ai, one man eventually stood guilty before God—his name was Achan. Though God had said, "Take no plunder," Achan had hidden silver and beautiful Babylonian clothing beneath his tent floor. He explained his failure in three phrases, "*I saw . . . I coveted . . . [I] took*" (Joshua 7:21, emphasis added). Those three steps can be used to explain the escalation of casual, chance encounters to adulterous relationships.

> T*he world judges its own people by their greatest accomplishments, but it judges God's people by their greatest moral failures.*

Achan's failing, "I saw . . . I coveted . . . [I] took" can certainly be applied to what happened to David. Everybody knows the story. David went to his rooftop in the cool of the evening and happened to see Bathsheba bathing. Yes, she was beautiful. Yes, David was intrigued. Yes, the king was accustomed to having what he wanted. But no, neither his DNA *nor* his urges were beyond his control. He coveted what was not his, for Bathsheba was the wife of Uriah, one of David's soldiers. He knew that, and he also knew the consequences which might follow a casual sexual relationship. And those consequences came to pass. Bathsheba eventually sent word to David that she was pregnant.

Then, David's adulterous relationship was compounded by murder as David engineered the death of Bathsheba's husband. If David had allowed things to continue in this vein, this would indeed be a tragic story, but instead, David rightly assumed full and complete responsibility for what he had done.

You may be thinking, "So what? This happened thousands of years in the past. Things are different today. People shack up all the time and it doesn't seem to be adversely affecting them." Even sociologists say, "Things are different now," that we don't need to adhere to these antiquated notions concerning infidelity. But talk to marriage counselors and pastors,

Insight

W*hile accurate statistics are difficult to come by (people are less than honest in confessing their failures) the reality is that almost always infidelity is a death sentence to a marriage.*

even bartenders, and they will tell you that the consequences of infidelity have not changed. Infidelity is almost always a death sentence to a marriage.

But it doesn't have to be. There are steps you can take to turn around a relationship that has gone sour. Recently, a radio talk show host, perhaps striving to find something to rivet the attention of his listeners, invited callers to deal with the issue of who is responsible when adultery takes place. The other person—usually the other woman? The wife who has been indifferent to the needs of her husband, or vice versa? Or the person who initiates the relationship?

No matter how indifferent your mate or how troubled your marriage may be, you—not someone else—are responsible for yourself, your choices and the consequences which inevitably follow. "I have sinned" (see Psalm 51:4) acknowledged David, and with that confession, the process of forgiveness and restoration began. It's the only way back.

Think on This

1. If you are ever tempted to have an affair, realize that in time your sin will find you out, and that it always comes with consequences.
2. If you are tempted and you pause for even an instant to consider taking the risk of infidelity, your marriage is in trouble. Get help now.
3. Is it necessary to "confess" your thoughts? Your actual failures? Why or why not?

Resource Reading
2 Samuel 11

David's Confession

"Create in me a pure heart, O God,
 and renew a steadfast spirit within me.
Do not cast me from your presence
 or take your Holy Spirit from me.
Restore to me the joy of your salvation
 and grant me a willing spirit, to sustain me."
(Psalm 51:10-12)

Grace is getting what you don't deserve, justice is getting exactly what you deserve and mercy is not getting what you really deserve. David knew that, and that is why, following his affair with Bathsheba, he pled for God's mercy. "Have mercy on me, O God, according to your unfailing love; according to your great compassion blot out my transgressions" (Psalm 51:1).

Those are the opening words of David's prayer found in Psalm 51, which provides the background for this and the following two selections. David's lament is the most emotion-laden and yet tender plea for forgiveness for the sin of infidelity in all literature—both secular and biblical.

David begins by assuming full responsibility for what happened. When confronted by Nathan, David immediately confessed, "I have sinned!" One commentator put it: "There is no evasion of responsibility . . . on the grounds of chance circumstance or an instinctive urge; no blaming of ignorance, necessity or evil agency; no attempt to make Bathsheba share the guilt of adultery and murder."[21]

"Wash away all my iniquity and cleanse me from my sin" (51:2) David cries out. Millions today, striving to come back following an adulterous relationship, lack what David felt: genuine repentance and sorrow for wrongdoing. That's much different from feeling bad that you got caught, or being embarrassed by the gossip that has gone the rounds. The verbs that David used speak of the depth of emotional feeling in his heart. They include, *blot out, wash, cleanse, create, renew, restore* and *save*—all powerful words which speak of forgiveness and cleansing.

Grace is getting what you don't deserve, justice
is getting exactly what you deserve and mercy is
not getting what you really deserve.

There are eight separate petitions in David's prayer. He begins by praying, "Cleanse me with hyssop, and I will be clean"(51:7). Hyssop was a brush-like plant used to sprinkle blood on the doorframes during Passover, a practice that began in Egypt. Then he says, "Wash me, and I will be whiter than snow." There were two words in Hebrew which could have been used for "wash." One means a simple washing such as you would apply to a dirty dish or pan. The other was the word used in reference to a soiled garment which you take down to the river and beat on the rocks until the stain comes out entirely. It was this word that David used. Isaiah later wrote, "Though your sins are like scarlet, they shall be as white as snow; though they are red as crimson, they shall be like wool" (Isaiah 1:18).

Knowing that there was no singing or joy in the home injured by an affair, David asks, "Let me hear joy and gladness" (Psalm 51:8). He continues, "Hide your face from my sins and blot out all my iniquity" (51:9). There's an interesting thing here. David called it what it is—not a moral failure, not a poor choice, not a mistake—but *sin*, us-

Insight

Human nature never changes; neither does the hand of the Lord grow heavy or His ear deaf to the cries of those who sincerely want His mercy, help and forgiveness.

ing the terminology which God uses, the only one for which there is forgiveness. Be done with the psychological babble that refuses to recognize adultery as nothing less than sin, first against God, as David recognized it, then against our wives, our husbands, our children and ourselves as well.

"Create in me a pure heart . . . and renew a steadfast spirit" (51:10), he asks, realizing that the issues of life, including temptation and how we deal with it, stem from the heart.

Then David asked that God would not cast him away from His presence or take away His Holy Spirit, but restore again the joy of His salvation. And did God answer David's prayer? Yes, He did! David wrote, "But there is forgiveness with thee, that thou mayest be feared" (Psalm 130:4, KJV).

If you find yourself in an adulterous relationship and want healing and help, don't bother with a counselor who will tell you, "Just get on with your life." Take the path less traveled which David describes in Psalm 51. There you will find God's therapy and His program for healing.

Think on This

1. A billboard in Manila, Philippines gets your attention with the statement, "Men think of women every 5.8 minutes." Whether or not the statement is factual or simply intended to grab attention is unclear; however, it does pose a question to be considered. If God should judge you for your thoughts (whether you are male or female), would you be guilty of "mental adultery"?

2. Every man who has ever betrayed his wife (and usually every wife who has betrayed her husband) has first visualized or fantasized the reality. If you find yourself struggling with your thought life, you need to confess it (1 John 1:9) and bring your thought life into captivity to Jesus Christ (2 Corinthians 10:5).

3. Is there a correlation between your thought life and what you view or feed your mind on?

Resource Reading
Psalm 51

Finding Your Way Back from Infidelity

"But there is forgiveness with thee, that thou mayest be feared." (Psalm 130:4, KJV)

Finding your way back after an adulterous relationship is difficult, but it can be done. There's a road map which guides you when you recognize what a dreadful thing has happened and you sincerely want forgiveness, healing and—yes!—restoration with your spouse. The road map is found in Psalm 51, and David, the author, simply describes the components of restoration which he went through.

Analyzing this powerful road map to restoration, I see several guidelines, all of which are vitally necessary. David practiced each one.

Guideline #1: Assume full responsibility for your wrongdoing. David did. "I have sinned," he immediately confessed to Nathan the prophet. "My sin is ever before me," he wrote in Psalm 51:3 (KJV). Don't bother blaming your DNA, your office worker who seduced you or your spouse who was indifferent to your needs. The first step is to recognize you went wrong and you are the one who needs to come back. Make it personal. David called it "my sin" (51:2), "my transgressions" (51:3) and "my iniquity" (51:9).

Guideline #2: Confess your failure for what it is—sin. That's what David called it, and that's what it is, so don't use psychobabble, calling it "a wrong choice," or a "misdeed" or a "moral lapse." The Bible says there is forgiveness for our sins, but it doesn't include the euphemisms that allow us to squirm out from under the yoke of accountability.

To whom do we confess? First, says David, confession must be made to God because we first sin against Him. "Against thee, thee only, have I sinned" (51:4, KJV) he said. Whoa! But what about your wife, your husband, your children? They too figure in the equation of forgiveness and they have to be included in genuine confession. The Bible says, "He who covers his sins will not prosper, But whoever confesses and forsakes them will have mercy" (Proverbs 28:13, NKJV).

> T*he Bible says there is forgiveness for our sins, but it doesn't include the euphemisms that allow us to squirm out from under the yoke of accountability.*

Guideline #3: Break off the illicit relationship completely and forever. There is no hope for healing as long as you dance with wrongdoing. Again the Bible says, "If I regard iniquity [sin] in my heart, the Lord will not hear me" (Psalm 66:18, KJV).

Guideline #4: Guard against continued contact or exposure. If you have to change jobs, do it. If you have to move to a different neighborhood, start packing. If you value your marriage and your future, drastic steps may be necessary. Remember, turning your back on your commitment "till death us do part" was drastic; so may be the measures necessary to find your way back.

Insight

Failure to take drastic action in righting a wrong only allows it to fester and become more devastating in its ultimate consequences.

David's failure was initiated by the fact that he was in the wrong place at the wrong time. Sometimes you can't help being in the wrong place, but what you do—whether you hang around to see what might happen or turn and run—is your decision.

Guideline #5: Ask for forgiveness and healing. Ask both God and those who have been hurt, including the person you were intimate with, to forgive you. Will they forgive? That probably depends on your attitude. When you are genuine and sincere they will probably forgive just as God does, though it may be hard for them. This is a risk which *must* be taken.

Guideline #6: Forever guard your weakness. Call home if you are running late. Watch what you read, guard your heart and make sure you are never alone with someone of the opposite sex in a situation where you can be compromised.

The way back is not easy, but it is worthwhile. Bones that are broken can heal even stronger than before they were broken, and though it's tough it can happen with your marriage as well. Affairs never make a marriage better, but they may point out your weaknesses, your human failures, your insensitivity; and you can do something to rectify that, which will make your marriage stronger.

Think on This

1. Few individuals can cover their wrongs forever (eventually most are found out) but you can minimize the impact of your failure by following the guidelines outlined in this selection. Do you know someone—a pastor or a trusted friend—who can help you find your way back home?

2. My godly father-in-law, Guy Duffield, used to say that secret sins should be confessed secretly, private sins should be confessed privately and public sins should be confessed publicly. Is David's failure (definitely a public sin) different from those confronting us today?

Resource reading

Hosea 2

When You
Are Tempted

*"But remember this—the wrong desires that come
into your life aren't anything new and different.
Many others have faced exactly the same problems before you. And no temptation is irresistible.
You can trust God to keep the temptation from becoming so strong that you can't stand up against
it, for he has promised this and will do what he
says. He will show you how to escape temptation's power so that you can bear up patiently
against it."* (1 Corinthians 10:13, LB)

Your husband no longer notices you, but a
coworker does. Your marriage has lost its romance and you are beginning to wonder if it really is you
who is no longer attractive. When a friend calls you and
talks about how compassionate and caring you are, you
think, *At least* someone *appreciates me.* You have two cars,
three kids and life has become completely predictable.
You're thinking, *Is this all there is for me?* If any of these
thoughts have crossed your mind you are a candidate for
an affair.

"Oh, not me!" you may respond. Paul warned, "Therefore let him who thinks he stands take heed lest he fall" (1 Corinthians 10:12, NKJV). If you find yourself feeling neglected and—yes!—tempted, then heed the following guidelines.

Guideline #1: Realize an affair never solves marital problems; it compounds them. It produces deceit, dishonesty and guilt—plenty of it. Neither does it make a marriage without communication suddenly blossom and come alive. The three Rs of infidelity are as follows: First—*resentment.* You don't like the way you are treated. Your husband doesn't pay attention to you but he seems to notice other women. You don't like the fact that your husband spends more time playing basketball with his friends than he spends with you.

> T*he marriage you save is your own and it's worth saving, never sacrificing for a fling. Never!*

Resentment which is not dealt with or confronted leads to the second R—*rationalization.* "This is a way that I can get his attention, or get even with him." I've heard men say, "What difference does it make? My marriage is all washed up anyway." Rationalization is a thinly veiled attempt to justify what you know is wrong. Instead of confronting issues which need to be faced, you throw away what can be a good marriage for a one-night adventure or a flight into nowhere.

The third R is *rendezvous.* At first, you may only sit and talk, but in the wrong place, under the wrong provocation, with the wrong person, you often end up in the wrong bed.

Guideline #2: Understand that an affair may be exciting, but the odds are that it will destroy any possibility of salvaging a marriage. Do people end up marrying those with whom they have affairs? Occasionally, but usually

Insight

Those who fight fire with fire end up getting burned themselves!

not. Candidates for infidelity don't measure up to the same standard as someone you want to spend the rest of your life with.

Guideline #3: Acknowledge that it's no sin to be tempted; the sin comes in yielding to your temptation. But—and here is where you turn the corner—if you allow yourself to be in situations where you know you just might yield, you are setting yourself up for moral failure. First Thessalonians 5:22 says, "Abstain from all appearance of evil" (KJV). The Bible also says that with every temptation comes a way of escape (see 1 Corinthians 10:12-13).

Avoid working alone with the pretty single woman who is obviously on the lookout for someone. Take a friend with you. Realize others have faced the same issues which you are dealing with. Find out how they dealt with them.

Guideline #4: Become accountable to someone. Join a small group, a cell group or a study group. Tell someone what you are struggling with and ask for help.

Guideline #5: Watch what you feed your mind on and what you think about. Skip the soaps during the daytime. Forget the tabloids, the romance novels and other things that glorify infidelity and make it so attractive.

Guideline #6: Go to work on your own marriage. Commitment is a bridge across troubled waters, and when you make the decision to never, ever think of having an affair or walking out on your mate, it's amazing how your relationship goes to a new level of understanding. The marriage you save is your own and it's worth saving, never sacrificing for a fling. Never!

Think on This

1. You (a female) are invited to attend a conference with your boss who is a handsome single male. You would fly together, stay at the hotel together in separate rooms and be together as company representatives on the sales floor. Are you comfortable with this? Should this be of concern to your husband or is it just business?

2. Reverse the order. You are the male and are asked to take another employee with you—a gal who is single, quite attractive and lonely. Would you a) tell your boss that you are not comfortable with this situation (is that sexual discrimination?), b) refuse to go or c) go and strive to keep your distance from her?

3. Is just spending time with a business associate of the opposite sex risky when your marriage isn't very solid? Even if you have a good marriage? Or do you think it matters at all?

Resource Reading
1 Corinthians 10

It's *a* Sex-Saturateδ Worlδ Out There

"But a man who commits adultery lacks judgment; whoever does so destroys himself." (Proverbs 6:32)

My wife and I had just boarded a flight from Amsterdam to the U.S. Seated next to us was a young man, about twenty-five years of age. It was impossible not to notice the glossy cover of the magazine he picked up, which featured a beautiful girl clad in a bikini, with an admiring young man nearby. The caption was, "Sex on the beach!" The glamorous tropical setting made it seem so natural, so beautiful and so spontaneous; but what the magazine, the media and the message of our culture do not tell you is that *sex is not casual, it is not free and it is certainly not without consequences*—whether you are single or married.

For the couple who are committed to each other in marriage, sexual union is a sacred and beautiful celebration of love initiated by God in the Garden long ago. But outside of marriage a sexual relationship has ramifications which few ever come to grips with, especially those in the throes of passion, who think of it only as a recreational instinct which must be satisfied or an activity which is required if you want to keep your partner interested.

But what is the reality?

Fact #1: Nothing in all of life's relationships so embraces the totality of your emotions, your physical senses and even your spiritual life as does sexual intercourse. There is a bonding that takes place in any sexual relationship—especially for women—which is part of God's plan and purpose; but when it is abused by casual sex, the consequences wound you emotionally. No other relationship in life is as painful and difficult to overcome when it has to be ended.

Because we are created in the image of God, people are equipped with emotions and feelings which make them different from barnyard animals who follow their basic passions and instincts. Emotional bonding is not a product of evolutionary happenstance. It is part of God's purpose to insure the continuity of marriage, guaranteeing that eventually a mother and a father would be there for their children.

T*hose who live together before marriage are fifty percent more likely to see their marriage fail.*

Fact #2: The media makes premarital and extramarital relationships seem so common that one might assume that they are the norm. In the past forty years, our culture has undergone a sexual revolution, as traditional relationships have been superceded by short-term ones which are severely lacking in commitment. In 1953, Alfred Kinsey reported that fifty percent of all husbands were unfaithful by age forty. Though his research was questioned soon thereafter, others using more valid research methods eventually came to the same conclusion. The November 1981 issue of *Psychology Today* reported that "half of married men eventually commit adultery, and so do about one in five married women by the time they reach 45. . . . However, among younger women rates are going up to approach male rates." [22]

In 1960, no more than one in ten couples lived together without being married. Today, as many as fifty percent of all couples live together before joining in marriage—something which has produced instability in relationships and many fewer marriages.[23] Now that the great experiment has been running for forty years, it is a proven

Insight

Deciding ahead of time where you draw the line and what you will do in any given situation makes the moment of temptation much easier to cope with.

fact: it just doesn't work. Those who live together before marriage are fifty percent more likely to see their marriage fail.

Fact #3: Nothing does more to contribute to divorce than does infidelity. The reality is that nothing does more to tear apart a relationship which was cemented with commitment and purity and was publicly celebrated in marriage than does breaking that relationship through adultery. In most cases, infidelity destroys a marriage. Ask any marriage counselor, any pastor, anyone even remotely familiar with the field, and you'll hear the same story.

Fact #4: In spite of the challenge which infidelity brings to a relationship, there can be forgiveness and

healing. While infidelity in marriage usually results in divorce, a marriage can be saved. Difficult? Yes. Impossible? Not at all.

Think on This

1. One of the best things you can do for marriage insurance is to have fun together. This, of course, means that you need to be able to disengage from responsibilities and enjoy being with your husband or wife. What fun things do you do together?
2. Rarely, if ever, do I hear from a man who has been in touch with God on a daily basis, through time in the Word and prayer, and in touch with his wife (a good relationship) who has yielded to temptation. Making this personal, how is your relationship with God? How is your relationship with your spouse?

Resource Reading
Proverbs 6

Dealing with Guilt

"Therefore, there is now no condemnation for those who are in Christ Jesus." (Romans 8:1)

One of the most difficult things for individuals who have bargained with their consciences and come out losers is to get back on top of things. They need the means to break the often repeated cycle of temptation, failure and guilt. Take, for example, the person who wrote: "I was a Christian when I committed my great sin, and God forgave me, but I fell again and again, thinking each time I would not [do it] any more. Oh, please pray for me that I will be a strong, radiant Christian. I am so ashamed that I let Satan win so many times."

Another person wrote asking for our booklet *Guidelines for Peace of Mind* and then said, "I would appreciate your prayers. I've been witnessing to a woman I work with. After some time together we grew very close and have ended up in bed several times. I feel so guilty that I'm being such a lousy example for her. I have yet to see how I can continue to witness and still maintain a pure physical life. I know what I'm doing is an offense to a holy and righteous God. Any suggestions you have would be most welcome."

The real issue is not "Why are we so weak?" it is "What can we do to find God's forgiveness and the strength we need to conquer our weakness?" Here are several guidelines that will help you when you find yourself in a situation which you know is wrong but you cannot seem to overcome.

Guideline #1: Avoid situations which have the faintest possibility of temptation. I am convinced that this is the real failure which leads to repeated downfalls. If you have yielded to sexual sin and you have confessed it to God, do not allow yourself to be alone with that person ever again. If it means changing jobs, then it is better to change jobs than to fall prey to temptation. Do not meet for coffee or dinner at your house because you just want to "talk." "Abstain from all appearance of evil" (1 Thessalonians 5:22, KJV), wrote Paul a long time ago, and that advice is still valid today.

T*he real issue is not "Why are we so weak?" it is "What can we do to find God's forgiveness and the strength we need to conquer our weakness?"*

Guideline #2: Make sure that your emotions and your drives have been submitted to the lordship of Jesus Christ. Does that mean that they cease to exist, that God takes them out of your life and makes you an emotionless blob? Many people really think that. They equate the Christian life with the asceticism of the monastery, or drinking vinegar or wearing black. But these extremes are not necessary. When you mean business with God and are willing to submit your body and your emotions to the lordship of Christ, you then make it possible for those needs to be met completely and fully through marriage.

To a sex-saturated culture, Paul wrote First Corinthians, and his words provide guidelines for us today. "No temptation has seized you," he wrote, "except what is common to man. And God is faithful; he will not let you be tempted beyond what you can bear" (1 Corinthians

Insight

Asking God for forgiveness isn't enough. You've got to nail the door shut so you can't go back.

10:13). That is the answer: His strength and help, combined with an escape route that protects your weakness. It is the only real solution.

Guideline #3: Make sure that a sexual relationship is not merely a substitute for an emotional need that you have in your life. Like what? Every person has three basic emotional needs: 1) to give and receive love; 2) to feel worthwhile to yourself and to others; and 3) to know the boundaries of security, which include a spiritual relationship with your heavenly Father. Sexual relationships outside of marriage are often misaligned attempts to meet emotional needs, but they only compound the problem.

Guideline #4: Get on solid footing, spiritually. This includes an understanding of God's forgiveness and help. There is forgiveness for past sins, and there is His strength and help to rise above the guilt of yesterday's failures. Thank God! There is hope for tomorrow, which makes today worth living.

Think on This

1. St. Augustine, who had a sexual relationship with a prostitute, was going down the street one day when she accosted him from a distance, calling him by name. He called back, "That Augustine is dead; I am the new Augustine." Drawing the line and stepping across it, going public as he did, makes it much easier to close the door on what you know is wrong. How can you do this?

2. Burning the bridge behind you is the only way to keep from crossing again. So how does this transfer into life today? Getting rid of access to the Internet, cable TV or video?

Resource Reading
1 John 1

Part V

Men and Women
Are Different

"Marriage is the art of two incompatible
people learning to live compatibly."[24]
—James Hewett

Men and Women Don't Talk the Same

*"Simply let your 'Yes' be 'Yes,' and your 'No,'
'No'; anything beyond this comes from the evil
one." (Matthew 5:37)*

Men and women don't communicate the same way, contends sociologist Deborah Tannen, author of *You Just Don't Understand—Women and Men in Conversation*. The title of her book only certifies the obvious. Ever since the days of Adam and Eve women have been telling us that men and women don't speak the same language. Even scientists have been telling us that there are differences in brain patterns between men and women which affect our ability to communicate with each other. Again, no great surprise to women. One veteran of many unsuccessful bouts to get through to a noncommunicative husband wrote, with a stroke of resignation, "He has lazy speech muscles—that's all!"

So men and women don't communicate. What's new? Sociologist Deborah Tannen videotaped hundreds of hours of conversations between males and females. Analyzing the substance of those conversations she learned that men and women tend to approach communication from entirely different planes of reference.

For women, talking validates the worth of a relationship or what they are discussing. For men, having to talk about it is a symptom of a problem. Men never fix anything that is not broken; women feel that a relationship that is worth anything is worth discussing. Tannen writes, "A lot of men feel that a woman's insistence on talking things out is like a dog hanging on to a bone. But for women, talk is the glue that holds relationships together."[25]

Have you experienced difficulty in communicating with your mate or members of the opposite sex? Make note of the following guidelines that will help you better understand the problem and how to tackle it.

Deepest communication for women results in intimacy, but for men intimacy in communication is a threat to their masculinity.

Guideline #1: Remember that men most often communicate on the level of the physical; women from the level of emotions and feelings. Like the three layers or spheres which surround our earth, communication has three levels: 1) trivia (closest to where we are); 2) facts, which usually relate to our lives physically; and 3) emotions and feelings, which are subjective. Men usually reach the limits of their ability to communicate when they express facts, but women begin there and go from facts to emotions. The result: deepest communication for women results in intimacy, but for men intimacy in communication is a threat to their masculinity. Their vulnerability makes them uneasy.

Guideline #2: Remember that communication means something totally different to men than it does to women. When I ask men to rate themselves on a scale of one to ten as communicators, men almost always rate themselves three points above what their wives rated them.

Guideline #3: Every person has a need to communicate, so look for the level of communication which allows the most adequate expression. For men, it means opening up to vent emotions and feelings; for women, it means understanding that your husband may really be trying, even when his efforts seem insufficient.

Insight

W*hile knowing how to communicate may not be a matter of life and death, it is a matter of utmost importance in a marriage.*

Guideline #4: Realize communication skills can be learned no matter how you grew up or how deficient you may be as a communicator. Communication is a skill which can be acquired, provided you value a friendship or a relationship enough to work at it.

Guideline #5: Learn to pick up on nonverbal signals. There are a lot of them—more than 700,000 ways to communicate nonverbally, says a Harvard University sociologist. It is important to recognize nonverbal signals, but it is more important to learn how to say things verbally.

Guideline #6: Let your mate know your relationship is important and that you want to work on your communication skills. Charles Dickens gave good advice when he said, "Never close your lips to him to whom you have opened your heart."

Think on This

1. Sit down with your mate and rate each other's effectiveness as a communicator on a scale of one to ten. Then exchange your results.
2. Ask each other, "What can I do to be a more effective communicator?"
3. There are more resources on effective communication available today than ever before in both Christian and secular outlets. Take advantage of them. They will help you to reap dividends in business as well as in your marriage.

Resource Reading
1 Corinthians 13

Men and Women Listen Differently, You Bet!

"Anyone, then, who knows the good he ought to do and doesn't do it, sins." (James 4:17)

My husband just doesn't get it," is a complaint often heard from wives. And often they are right, but now they have scientific evidence to back up their allegations. Scientists, using a modified MRI unit (that's mirror resonance imaging), have taken pictures of both male and female brains that prove—are you ready for this?—that women use both sides of their brains when they listen, and men use only one side.[26] As one woman responded upon hearing the news, "One more excuse to get away with what they've been doing for ages: not paying attention to us." OK, now men have an excuse, shallow as it may be.

Since Adam discovered Eve in the garden, people have known that men and women are different, but *how* different they are is still a matter of scientific discovery. While social engineers try to wipe out the distinctions between males and females, everything that those researchers have discovered about the human brain and how it functions has flown in the face of the unisex emphasis.

We are genetically different. Scientists are now talking about "male brains" and "female brains." Your chemistry determines how you think, and how you think determines how you behave. And your chemistry is the result of having come from the drawing board of heaven as either uniquely male or female, not whether you played with dolls or cars when you were a baby, or whether your parents painted your room blue or pink.

But of all the differences that exist, none are more pronounced than how men and women communicate. We know for a fact that the left side of the brains of prenatal female babies begins to develop sooner than the left side of prenatal male babies. And, as you probably suspect, it is the left side of the brain that primarily controls your speech— which means little girls talk sooner than little boys and also talk a lot more over their lifetimes. The average female uses 30,000 words a day while the average male uses about 20,000. That means females can speak at an average of sixty miles an hour with bursts to eighty or ninety miles per hour while males putt along at about forty miles an hour.

M*en and women are different, and only by recognizing this can our deep needs be met.*

We know, however, that it isn't just how many words are spoken but how men and women listen and communicate that is different. Women use both sides of their brains when they listen; men use mostly the left side.

Does this give men a valid excuse for not listening when their wives talk? Not for a minute—though it may explain why women tend to be intuitive and pick up on nonverbal signals which we men completely miss. One of the most important things that men can do for women is to listen—

not try to fix the problem, not try to watch TV or read the sports section at the same time they listen with one ear, but to give complete and undivided attention to the one who is sharing her heart with them.

No man can really love his wife without meeting her needs, and one of the greatest of all our needs is to have someone who loves us really listen to us, giving us his or her complete and undivided attention.

Insight

At the very time when social scientists have been trying to convince us that men and women are all the same (unisex), researchers in the laboratory are demonstrating what the Bible has been telling us: We are different, and those God-ordained differences are part of His equipping us to fill different roles in life.

Understanding sexual differences doesn't provide an excuse for our failure but should underline the importance of knowing that communication means something completely different to men than it does to women.

It used to be that the context of communication between the sexes was, "He said, she said," but now it's "he heard, she heard. No, he really didn't hear, but she did."

Chalk one up for scientific research in confirming what the Bible has said for centuries—men and women are different, and only by recognizing this can our deep needs be met.

Think on This

1. Putting down the newspaper, hitting the "mute" button on the remote and looking at someone as you listen to what is being said is not only a matter of

common courtesy, it's vital if you are going to hear what is being said. Do you practice this? a) Sometimes, b) Most of the time, c) Honestly—never! Are you willing to give it a try for just ten days?

2. OK, it's a fact. Women listen better than men do (they talk better as well). So is this an excuse men can make to cover for not listening?

3. If communication consists of having things heard rather than just saying them, is the cycle of communication complete when either person involved in a conversation doesn't really hear?

Resource Reading
Philippians 2:1-4

Men and Women Think Differently Too

"For this reason a man will leave his father and mother and be united to his wife, and they will become one flesh." (Genesis 2:24)

Take a minute and see how well your brain is working. Wiggle your right toe. OK—it was the left side of your brain which kicked in and told it to move. Now take both hands and put them on opposite shoulders and move your fingers. Now your hands are on the same side of your brain which gives them the order to move. Got it? The right side of your brain controls the left side of your body, and vice versa.

Your brain is divided into two hemispheres which are connected with nerve fibers. If you are female, before you were born the left side of your brain began to develop earlier than the right side of the brain of little male babies. And what does the left side of your brain control, in addition to motor ability on the ride side of your body? Your ability to talk, to read and to verbalize thoughts. "We use the left side of the brain," says one authority on human development, "when we read a newspaper, sing a song, play bridge, or write a letter."[27]

In real life this translates to a female's ability to talk circles around the males in her life. There's a reason, men, why women are more prone than you to have wind erosion on their teeth and get calluses on their vocal chords. Talking is the natural expression of their natures.

What about the right side of the brain, what does it control? We use the right side of the brain "when we consult a road map, thread our way through a maze, work a jigsaw puzzle, design a house, plan a garden, recognize a face, paint a picture, possibly when we listen to music, definitely when we solve a problem in geometry," says Dr. Joyce Brothers.[28]

God made both men and women in His image and equipped them to do tasks which complement each other.

This means that the right side of the brain helps you see the large picture. It also accounts for more than a few arguments between men and women. Example: You are traveling and your husband is driving the car. You as a woman notice that nothing looks familiar. The conversation goes something like this:

"Joe, do you know where we are?"

He answers, "Of course I do."

"Come on, Joe, nothing looks familiar. Let's stop and ask directions."

He says, "I don't need to ask directions. I can get us where we need to go."

You say, "Admit it. We're lost and you don't know where we are."

He rebuts, "Sure I do."

In reality you are both right. He conceptualizes, seeing the larger picture (hopefully), and you intuitively look for details which tell you that he doesn't know precisely where you are. Can you relate to what I have just described?

Insight

I*n a marriage, each has what the other needs and can never find apart from coming together in marriage.*

The fact that the right side of the brain is also used to do math explains why males tend to be better at math and science than women are, though there are exceptions to every generalization.

Does this mean that men are better than women? Using the term "better than" implies superiority, but the reality is that we are *different*. Each sex is unique, and that uniqueness means men and women have strengths and weaknesses in different areas.

Understanding the differences helps to bring harmony and eliminate competition. Function is the result of design. Instead of trying to force men and women into the same mold, it is high time that we recognize what Moses knew 3,000 years ago. God made both men and women in His image and equipped them to do tasks which complement each other. Knowing what those differences are and respecting them are the keys to harmony and happiness.

Think on This

1. What are your strengths? What are your mate's strengths?

2. If both men and women are equipped with different abilities, wouldn't our relationships be stronger if we played off each other's strengths and weaknesses instead of competing with each other?
3. Do you find it difficult not to say, "I told you so! You should have listened to me!" when your husband finally admits that you are lost?

Resource Reading
Genesis 3:17-24

Never Call 'Em the Weaker Sex

*"Then the LORD God made a woman from the
rib he had taken out of the man, and he brought
her to the man.*
The man said,

*'This is now bone of my bones
and flesh of my flesh;
she shall be called "woman,"
for she was taken out of man.' "*
(Genesis 2:22-23)

Who said that women are the weaker sex?
Strength or weakness is merely a matter of
definition. It's true that men have about thirty percent
greater upper body strength, and that their bulk is about
forty-one percent muscle compared to women's having
thirty-five percent muscle. That's why men who lift
weights tend to bulk up while women who do the same
thing obtain firm muscle tone but still retain a softness and
more of an hourglass figure. Like it or not, that's the way
God made us, and our bodies respond to a genetic blueprint
which was formulated at the moment of conception.

But from that point on it's downhill for us men! For every 100 girl babies which come into the world, there are 105 to 107 boy babies, yet who are the ones who cash in the insurance policies after the three-score-and-ten years?[29] Women! They consistently outlive men. Boy babies sustain one-third more birth defects, and despite the fact that it is males who want to show off and do dangerous things, it's the females who have a physical stamina which keeps them alive when their male counterparts don't make it.

Of the fifteen leading causes of death, men lead the pack in fourteen of those, including death from heart attacks, strokes, cancer and a miscellaneous assortment of other devastating illnesses.

T*he differences between men and women are*
God-ordained differences intended to equip
both sexes to accomplish roles which
produce harmony and happiness.

When women have strokes and the right side of their body is affected, they are far more prone to regain fluency than men. Women get the same physical problems as men, but they usually weather them much better. Take high blood pressure, for example. Women struggle with high blood pressure more than men do, but they usually don't die from it. For every four men with high blood pressure, there are five women with the disease. "Men don't tolerate it as well," says Dr. John Laragh of the New York Hospital-Cornell Medical Center. "The truth is," he says, "that men don't tolerate anything as well as women."[30]

There is another barometer of strength—emotional strength, and this is the one that you don't find on the charts; but a long time ago, I came to the conclusion that women are stronger than men when it comes to handling emotional stress, especially death. When a woman loses her husband, she cries and grieves, but then she regroups and picks up the pieces of her life and moves on. When men face the loss of a spouse, they grieve but often never really regain their emotional equilibrium.

OK, what's the bottom line? Does that make women stronger than men? That question will never truly be answered, but there is one truth which our generation needs to confront. *The differences between men and women are God-ordained differences intended to equip both sexes to accomplish roles which produce harmony and happiness.*

The sad thing is that the quest for equality, which demands that men and women be recognized as having been cut from the same pattern, denies the sexual differences which make for real happiness and harmony.

When an Anglican minister who was quite far-sighted was asked to marry a couple who had bought into the unisex concept, he came to the line in the wedding ceremony when the groom was asked to kiss the bride. He adjusted his half-frame glasses and noticed that both of the two who stood before him had long hair, both individuals had earrings hanging from their ears and he honestly couldn't tell by looking which was the groom.

Insight

Sexual differences are all part of God's design and plan, and when we cooperate with the Architect in recognizing that there is a difference, both men and women achieve greater satisfaction in life than when we fight against the blueprint.

Finally, he cleared his throat and said, "Would one of you please kiss the bride?" I just hope that the two who got married really knew the difference.

Think on This

1. Some of the ancient rabbis thanked God that they were neither Gentiles nor women. Their wives, however, having become widows, surely thanked God that they were women, having outlived their men. Do you rejoice in being who you are, a unique individual created in the image of God? How much does your sex really matter?

2. Both men and women were created for a purpose. Recognizing this helps us understand who we are. If someone asked you, "Who are you?" how would you answer?

Resource Reading
Genesis 3:1-16

The Marriage Saver of Communication

"Anyone, then, who knows the good he ought to do and doesn't do it, sins." (James 4:17)

Y ou can count on it every time: When there is a problem in a marriage or a relationship, the problem includes a failure to communicate. Whether it is thoughts, feelings or perspectives on certain situations, it is a failure to communicate something that is vital to the health of the relationship. It is an old problem which has been compounded in recent days by our culture and our sometimes unrealistic expectations in marriage.

Interested in saving your marriage or making a good marriage better? Then make communication a priority! As the result of working with people from different cultures for many years, I am absolutely convinced that communication skills *can be learned*. I am also convinced that most people, especially men, think they are better at communication than they really are.

Effective communication is not yelling or screaming at another person—that may work when a house is on fire, but it just doesn't fly in a marriage. Much of what we think is communication really falls into the category of what Shakespeare described in Macbeth as, "Full of sound and fury but signifying nothing!" Communication—the kind that makes a marriage work—is opening the windows of your heart and allowing another to see within, as you strive to express your ideas, feelings, thoughts, emotions and ideas without intimidation.

There are two major problems with communication today: 1) Many of us think we are communicating in marriage when the other spouse says, "No—you are not!" And 2) Communication means something totally different to men and women, which means that there is—very definitely—a male language and a female one, even though they use the same vocabulary.

I*nterested in saving your marriage or making a good marriage better? Then make communication a priority!*

"Dear Dr. Sala," wrote a friend of *Guidelines*, "please pray for us. My husband filed for divorce and moved out. He won't discuss the situation so I don't know why he wants a divorce; he just says he doesn't want to be married any longer. After twelve years I thought we were getting along pretty well. There was no warning at all!"

Did you notice that last phrase, "There was no warning at all!"? This phrase so aptly describes the problem. Men and women use different languages when they communicate. In a previous selection I pointed out that men communicate from a rational or logical point of reference (the factual level); women from an emotional reference. Men (though not all of them) tend to think; women tend to feel. Men are generally pretty deficient at nonverbal communication; women are generally masters at it. Men accept things at face value; women are sensitive and pick up nonverbal signals that are often completely lost on men.

Insight

The longer you wait to learn communication skills the more difficult it becomes.

Understanding how important communication is, what can a couple do to communicate better in marriage?

Guideline #1: Strive to say what you mean and mean what you say. Effective communication isn't a matter of saying something; it is a matter of having something heard. "I said that." "No you didn't." "Yes, I did!" No matter what you said, if the other hasn't heard, you *haven't communicated!*

Guideline #2: Develop the habit of listening. How? By concentrating on what you are hearing, not what you are saying, by rephrasing what you hear and by asking questions for clarification.

Guideline #3: Set the stage for communication. Take time when you are not busy or exhausted. Perhaps you need to make a date with your spouse so that you will have uninterrupted time to communicate with each other.

Guideline #4: Look at the issue from the other's point of view. You can win the argument (and a lot of men do) and subsequently lose your love.

Guideline #5: Communicate about what's important to you! Communication can save your marriage or make a good marriage even better. It's the key to real happiness.

Think on This

1. When you think that you are not being heard, try to re-phrase what you said or suggest that the other person rephrase what he or she heard.
2. Take time to unwind—have a cup of coffee, take a walk through the woods or in the park, turn off the TV and relax. Only then can you begin to dig down into the re-cesses of your thoughts and let them out. Deep and ef-fective communication can't be scheduled into a spare thirty minutes here and there.

Resource Reading

Philippians 4:4-9

Choosing to Succeed as a Communicator

"If I speak in the tongues of men and of angels, but have not love, I am only a resounding gong or a clanging cymbal." (1 Corinthians 13:1)

Men and women have always had difficulty communicating, and now we know why—at least to a very small degree. It's a proven fact that women listen with both sides of their brains, while men listen primarily with one side. But what we've known for ages is still true: though it may be a challenge, communicating can be done. I am convinced that communication is the key to any relationship, whether it is your marriage, getting along with your neighbor or succeeding in business.

The following are guidelines that will help you find an interested listener when you need to express something.

Guideline #1: Choose the right time. A pastor friend of mine tells how a deacon would often confront him just as he was ready to walk out on the platform for the service and say, "Pastor, I don't care what they are saying about you, I still love you." Wrong timing. When the one you need to communicate with is tired, busy or under stress, that's not the right time to try to talk with him or her. Women tend to want to communicate late in the day when men are physically weary; remember to choose your timing wisely.

Guidelines #2: Choose the right place. Arguing in front of your children is wrong (period!) no matter how good it may make you feel to get something off your chest. Kids can get caught in the crossfire and become emotionally wounded. They don't want to choose between Mommy's side or Daddy's side. Relaxing at the end of the day over a cup of coffee is a far better time to talk about the in-laws' visit than when your husband walks through the door after having been on a business trip for the last three days.

I *am convinced that communication is the key to any relationship, whether it is your marriage, getting along with your neighbor or succeeding in business.*

Guideline #3: Choose the right words. This means that you should think about how you would respond if you heard what you are going to say. Some words are inflammatory and guaranteed to produce an argument. Other words are conciliatory. "I" statements rather than "you" statements are less pointed. Describing your feelings is better than attacking the person.

Guideline #4: Choose the right attitude. How do you do this? Pray about your concern. Then think through the implications. How important is it for you to win every round? Think through the importance of what you want. Some issues are just not important enough to be issues, so ask yourself, "How will I feel about this in a year? In a month? Even next week?"

One study on communication between husbands and wives indicated that when husbands didn't listen, no wife really liked it, but when she knew that her husband really loved her, the marriage survived—sometimes battered and less than perfect, but when a husband didn't listen and the wife was convinced that she wasn't loved, the marriage often failed.

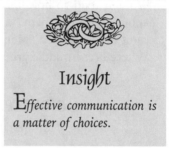

Insight

Effective communication is a matter of choices.

Guideline #5: Choose the right volume. A lot of folks mistakenly think that turning up the volume makes them more effective as a communicator. But it merely inflates their blood pressure—not good for either party. When I travel internationally, I often encounter people who don't understand what another person is saying, so they simply repeat the same question or say the same thing, getting louder and louder with each unsuccessful attempt. This method doesn't work in a foreign country or in a marriage.

Effective communication doesn't consist of saying things but of having things heard; so when you say something, don't just assume that the other person has heard or understands what you have said. Sometimes saying it again, another way, gets through the fog and sometimes saying, "OK, let's go back over what we've decided," is sufficient to help you understand that what you said is not what the other person heard. Got it? Good. Now we're communicating.

Think on This

1. Your husband has been on a business trip and walks through the door. You hit him with some pretty heavy stuff and he reacts negatively. How could your timing have been better?
2. Women tend to hold on to things they need to talk about, stuffing them inside themselves until they can't hold any more. Men tend to just blurt them out. Where is the middle ground for both?

Resource Reading
Philippians 4:1-9

The Silent Husband

"But anyone who won't care for his own relatives when they need help, especially those living in his own family, has no right to say he is a Christian. Such a person is worse than the heathen." (1 Timothy 5:8, LB)

The Vatican library is said to contain two Bibles. One Bible is two feet thick while the other has only a few pages in it. The first is said to contain everything that Eve said to Adam; the other, what Adam said to Eve! The pundit who came up with that story may not be too accurate in the details, but it does point up a real problem: It is more difficult for husbands to share their thoughts and to express themselves than it is for their wives, and it's been that way from the beginning of time.

The problem of communication between husbands and wives is further compounded by the fact that men and women view communication from entirely different vantage points. In general, men view communication in terms of facts while women view it in terms of emotions.

Quite often men think that they have communicated with their wives when actually their wives complain, "My husband will not talk to me." Communication is more than a few simple nods of the head or one-word answers in response to a question or two. It is the total sharing of a life which involves your thoughts, ideas, emotions and attitudes, in addition to the information that you pass on in the course of living together.

Most wives can suffer through a communication blackout during football or basketball season, but what really gets them down is when the lines of communication are not restored during the off-season. I am thinking of the wife who complained, "It's heartbreaking! Before we were married we would talk for hours at a time. Both of us talked—not just me. When we go out together now, we sit there and hardly exchange a dozen words. What has happened?" After a couple has been married for a few years, weariness and boredom can set in and they may stop talking and start giving signals. They begin taking each other for granted.

> Good communication isn't a matter of life and death; it's more important than that.

Another reason for this communication blackout is fear. Though he may not admit it, there are times when a husband is afraid to really open up. He may have tried it before and his wife's superior logic really put him down. What did he do? Did he fly off the handle and scream? Probably not. Instead he made a mental note. The next time that he saw a discussion on the horizon, he would just sail around it and avoid a verbal encounter. He was really afraid of talking with his wife about anything that was close to his heart.

Criticism is another communication stopper. A husband tells his wife about something that happened at work. Then his wife begins to criticize his actions. "Surely you didn't sit there and take that, did you?" How does he respond next time? He just does not bother to tell her what happened.

Insight

Before I can love you, I've got to know you, and before I can really know you, I've got to be able to communicate with you; therefore, communication is a prerequisite to love and is necessary to sustain and perpetuate it.

Closely akin to the wife who criticizes her husband is the one who gives him unasked for advice, especially when she does not really have all of the facts. Suppose a man has three employees. There is a problem with one employee but he is still a good man. However, his wife is convinced that he ought to be fired and says so, loud and clear. The next time, her husband is not at all sure that he wants to tell her about things at work lest it cause conflict between them.

Other husbands find it difficult to talk with their wives because they are afraid of the tears which sometimes come as a reaction to what they say. They do not know how to handle tears. They feel guilty and come apart inside when a wife starts crying. As a result, they avoid confrontations.

Fears and frustrations have to be recognized and dealt with, but they can be overcome. Communication is a two-way street. Learning to share your emotions or feelings is a great step toward a happy and successful marriage. Good communication isn't a matter of life and death; it's more important than that.

Think on This

1. Is there a "best time" for you to communicate with someone you love?
2. Is it true that "absence makes the heart grow fonder"? Can you be separated and keep your relationship alive without ongoing communication?
3. Do you consider the Internet and e-mail to be a boon to communication or a threat to it? What has it been in your household?

Resource Reading
Ephesians 5:21-33

You Think You Know Your Husband, Do You?

"The man said,

'This is now bone of my bones
   and flesh of my flesh;
she shall be called "woman,"
   for she was taken out of man.' "
(Genesis 2:23)

So you think you know your husband, do you? Well, you may very well be right. The fact is, you probably know him much better than he knows you. But we're just going to test you a little to see just how well you do know him. In the next selection, your husband is going to take a short quiz about you, but now it's your turn. Answer as many of the following questions as you can:

1. Does the man in your life still have his tonsils? If not, how old was he when he had them removed?
2. Within five pounds, how much does your husband weigh? Or for a variation, do you think he knows how much you weigh, within the same range of variation?
3. How many keys are on your husband's key ring? (If you're within a couple of the actual number, consider it a right answer.)

4. What's your husband's shoe size?
5. If your husband raided the refrigerator at midnight to make himself a sandwich, would he cut it into a rectangle, a triangle or just eat it whole?
6. If your husband found a fellow employee stealing from his employer, would he a) do nothing at all, b) tell the employer, c) help himself to a bit of the booty?
7. If your husband won a prize or inherited a small fortune, would he a) quit working, b) keep on doing the same thing, or c) do something entirely different?
8. When is the last time your husband prayed with you? Or prayed by himself?
9. If your husband could do one thing to change you, what would he do?
10. If your husband should die and stand knocking at heaven's door, and an angel should say, "Why should I let you in?" what would he say? (Ouch! Did I touch on a sensitive spot?)

I*ntimacy in marriage is far more than what takes place behind the bedroom door.*

Three questions were physical, and about the same number were social and several were spiritual in nature. Do you really know the man that you married? Does he really know you? Or do you both live in the same household day after day, month after month, year after year and play games? Intimacy in marriage is far more than what takes place behind the bedroom door. It is sharing your likes and dislikes, your thoughts and fancies, your desires and even the spiritual burdens of your heart. Of course there are dangers, and because of this some folks find it risky to really open up. There's always the danger of being misunderstood or considered eccentric. It is generally far more difficult for men to reveal feelings and emotions than for women. Challenged by the fear of rejection, men hide things—at least, they think they hide them.

Insight

Knowing details about someone doesn't necessarily mean that you know that person, but the more time you spend together and the more intimate you are with each other (not just sexually) the better you will really know each other.

There is the possibility of rejection, of being thought odd or different, but when you really love someone and he loves you, intimacy is the glue that makes you one in thought and spirit as well as in body. "For this reason," says the Bible, "a man will leave his father and mother and be united to his wife, and they will become one flesh" (Genesis 2:24). That is the beautiful relationship that God intends—the kind that you can have if you are willing to work at it.

Intimacy involves three definite areas: your body, your mind and your spirit—corresponding to the physical, the emotional and the spiritual. If you don't touch each other at all three levels, you do not really have all there is. Believe me, there is a price to intimacy, but it's well worth the cost and effort.

Think on This

1. For a week, without saying anything about what you're doing, observe what your husband eats, what he wears, what he says and then see how many things you learn about him.

2. Does your husband have difficulty expressing his feelings? Do you? Does it help when you ask, "What are you thinking about?" Or ask, "Would you like to talk? I'd be glad to listen."

Resource Reading
Genesis 24

You Think You Know Your Wife, Do You?

"Be very careful, then, how you live—not as unwise but as wise, making the most of every opportunity, because the days are evil." (Ephesians 5:15-16)

Y ou think you know your wife, do you? Well, how about taking a few moments to answer ten questions. You may not know as much as you think do. Try to answer the following questions:

1. What is her favorite perfume?
2. When she has a headache, does she take one aspirin or two? Or something else, or nothing?
3. Name two fairly common foods which she cannot stand.
4. If she has been with her best friend who shared a juicy bit of gossip with her, would she tell you?
5. Which of these can she not do? a) touch her toes? b) do a headstand? c) add a quart of oil to the family car?
6. What size shoe does she wear?
7. Would she rather have spaghetti or pizza?

8. Has she read a good book in the past month? If so, what is the title?
9. Would she read the front page of a newspaper before turning to the women's section?
10. If given a choice, would she rather spend an evening at a good movie or at a concert?

If you didn't know the answer to some of the above questions, sit down and discuss those questions with your wife—you'll find out the answers and hopefully spend some quality time communicating.

We often think we know each other when, in fact, we fail to see much beyond the surface and often do not even see that. (If you doubt that, then tell me what your wife was wearing when you left the house this morning.) Communication, though, is far more than merely cataloging likes and dislikes; it is seeing beyond the exterior to the very heart of a person. It is a two-way street. All too often we know certain things *about* each other, but we don't actually *know* each other.

T*o communicate effectively you have to meet each other on the same level.*

The ten questions above are a reflection of knowledge, and you may have scored quite well on them. But having knowledge of someone is different than actually knowing someone. And apart from communication at a meaningful level we will never become more than intimate strangers, never going beneath the surface to get to where we really *know* each other.

I like to define communication as an exchange—both verbal and nonverbal—between two people. It is a mutual sharing of ideas, thoughts, attitudes, feelings, emotions and information. Actually, it is all of that plus a great deal more. To communicate effectively you have to meet each other on the same level. If one of you takes the superior attitude and talks down to the other, then you are not communicating effectively. By the same token, if you consider yourself to be inferior to the other, you will find it hard to feel at ease and your communication with each other will suffer.

Insight

Men who are fixers by nature are often frustrated by women who tell them what is on their minds, yet women often don't want men to fix things—merely to listen to them.

One of the greatest barriers to communication is the refusal to accept another person just as he or she is. We try, instead, to make that person into the kind of person we would like him or her to be.

By the way, how did you do on those ten questions? If you scored nine or ten right, then you are superior in your knowledge of your wife, if you scored seven or eight, then you are average. If you scored below seven, then you had better start paying attention.

Commitment and communication are the two golden keys to a fruitful marriage. Without them, no marriage can succeed for very long. You must make the commitment and you *must* learn to communicate. But remember, apart from commitment there is no meaningful communication.

Think on This

1. Seldom do men pick up on the nonverbal signals which women send that include attitudes, moods and feelings. Can you tell when she is having a low day emotionally? Do you ever ask, "Honey, how did your day go? I'd like to hear about it."
2. A man who says he can read his wife like a book only shows how ignorant he really is. What is he missing which he should have gotten?

Resource Reading

Ephesians 5:1-21

Why Am I Afraid to Tell You Who I Am?

"When Jesus saw Nathanael approaching, he said of him, 'Here is a true Israelite, in whom there is nothing false.' " (John 1:47)

W hy am I afraid to tell you who I really am, what I really think and feel? I'm afraid that you will reject me. Being accepted is very important, so I put on this front and try to make you think I'm something I wish I were but I'm really not.

Almost everyone feels this way at some time or another. But when it comes to being vulnerable, it is very often men who must struggle with the issue, and their often clumsy attempts to hide their feelings are resented by the women in their lives.

The fact is, what most men are afraid to really give—intimacy—is what women want most out of marriage. I'm not talking about the hushed whispers of a husband and wife in the privacy of their bedroom; I'm talking about opening the window shades of your heart and letting the person closest to you know what really lies within—all the boogeymen and creepy crawlers of fear and incompetence that you think are there. Men, contrary to what you think, she'll love you all the more if you are willing to run the risk of letting her know exactly how you feel.

A simple, practical definition of intimacy can be made by breaking down the components of the English word "intimacy," as "into me see," which means allowing someone to look within your heart to see precisely what is there. This definition of intimacy can be applied to our relationship with God as well as our relationships with each other.

There are many people who have attempted to be vulnerable with someone else, and they have been betrayed. So they pull in the bridges and push others away, not wanting to run the risk of betrayed confidence and potential hurt. These people are the unfortunate ones who become prisoners to their own fears. It is far better to love and lose, than to never love at all.

Т*he fact is, what most men are afraid to really give—intimacy—is what women want most out of marriage.*

What are the ingredients that go into the kind of intimacy that allows others to look within our hearts to see who we really are?

Ingredient #1: Meaningful communication. This is the exchange of thoughts and ideas in an open forum. This goes well beyond the factual level of communication to a level that is based in emotions and feelings. Men, you need to realize that your wives are not just interested in what you *think* about something. They want to know how you *feel* about it.

Ingredient #2: Vulnerability. You've got to overcome the risk attached to being yourself and nothing more. Strangely, this also applies to your relationship with God, who knows you and loves you as you are. When someone really loves another that love extends to ideas and concepts which may be different from his or her own. Accepting someone who is your mirror image isn't love at a very deep level.

Insight

*W*hile men fear that if they are completely open and honest with their wives they will reject them, the very opposite is true. Women will accept and love them even more deeply.

Ingredient #3: Acceptance without censure. This means that love is unconditional. It has no strings attached. It isn't bartered for something that you want. It means that you don't push someone away when he or she doesn't give you the instant answers that you expect.

Ingredient #4: Complete honesty. In a recent interview I had regarding my book *When Friends Ask for Help* I was asked why I said my wife was my best counselor over the years. In one sentence, I replied, "Because she balances love with complete honesty!" Complete honesty allows for greater intimacy and trust, which are things we all must strive for in our relationships.

Ingredient #5: Sensitivity. Women are sensitive on many levels and in general that sensitivity makes them much better at intimacy than men. Can men learn from women in this regard? You bet they can. One key to sensitivity is picking up on nonverbal signals so that you give a person the freedom to open up and share when he or she is willing and so you know when not to push him or her.

Ingredient #6: Confidentiality. Almost nothing destroys trust more than betraying it. Some things should be kept in the drawer of your memory forever. Preserving them in such a manner becomes the glue that makes your past only the prelude to the future.

Applying these ingredients for intimacy to your relationship is well worth the time and the effort. Try it; you'll like the dividends it brings.

Think on This

1. Do you as a male confuse "pillow talk" with intimacy? Intimacy is nonsexual. It is being completely open, honest and vulnerable. Do you fear rejection if you allow your wife that much access into your thinking?
2. Don't fall into the trap of thinking, "If you really loved me, you would know what I'm thinking." You have to say it and spell it out so the other clearly understands. Real intimacy is spontaneous and can be unguarded so you let the other see deeply within.

Resource Reading
Colossians 3

What Women Most Want Out of Marriage

"Keeping a close watch on him, they sent spies, who pretended to be honest. They hoped to catch Jesus in something he said so that they might hand him over to the power and authority of the governor." (Luke 20:20)

He was a young seminarian who had just taken his first church. His wife was a talented, attractive woman and the young pastor seemed very capable. As we were talking, discussing some rather personal issues, he confided that he and his wife had never prayed together. This struck me as strange.

Here was a young man who believed in prayer; he led his congregation in prayer—at least on Sundays. He occasionally spoke on the subject of prayer in his sermons, but he and his wife had never made it a regular practice to clasp hands and pray together.

Responding, I asked, "Would you mind telling me why not?" Somewhat embarrassed, he said, "I've been afraid that if we prayed together, she would know how weak I am; how I struggle with things. I've been afraid that she wouldn't look up to me as a strong person!"

Strange, isn't it, how we think that our spouse will never know something when it is obvious to almost everyone but ourselves? The fact is that women can accept and love men far more deeply when men are vulnerable and honest. It's all part of an intimacy with each other which goes far, far beyond what men usually associate with the subject.

Intimacy is the openness to share your heart without fearing rejection or censure. It is accepting and embracing each other as we are, with wholehearted commitment. It is knowing the fears and pain of another without mocking. It is supporting the other emotionally, physically and spiritually. It is holding someone close and whispering, "It's OK," when logic cannot rise to do battle with emotions.

> The fact is that women can accept and love men far more deeply when men are vulnerable and honest.

Merle Shain, in his book, *Courage My Love*, says,

Intimacy is a haven where your vulnerabilities don't humiliate you, where sex is always warm and close, and all your funny lines are understood. It's knowing someone so well you can no longer tell where they begin and you leave off, as in the cartoon in which one old person says to another, 'Which one of us doesn't like broccoli?' It's an eye that catches yours across the room; it's pet names, and making plans, a cup of tea brought to bed. It's a hug when you need it and even when you don't; it's knowing you have a date for Saturday night.[31]

I've been thinking a great deal recently about intimacy in marriage, and my thoughts have gone from that to my relationship with God. What is necessary to forge a relationship of intimacy in marriage is also necessary to go beyond having just a formal relationship with God. If I am to enjoy the warmth of the relationship which God makes possible; if I would reach out to Him in the manner in which he

Insight

The individual who takes the risk of not being understood is often rewarded with far greater understanding and acceptance than he or she thought possible. Opening up to another person is both one of the most difficult and one of the most rewarding things you will ever do.

reaches out to me, what is necessary? Deep communication, which I can have by pouring out my heart in prayer.

Second, I need to be completely vulnerable. Why not? God already knows me. When I confess my sin and failure am I not being vulnerable? Am I not seeing life from His point of view?

Then there is acceptance without censure. "As a father pitieth his children, so the LORD pitieth them that fear him" (Psalm 103:13, KJV). God does not sternly rebuke my failures; He forgives and reaches out with strength to steady me as I learn to walk without falling.

Honesty, sensitivity and confidentiality are part of this relationship as well—all of which God has promised in His Word. Think about it, friend. It is all there as you trust Him.

Think on This

1. What does acceptance without censure mean to you? Does God receive us this way? (See Ephesians 4:32 as a pattern.)
2. If someone betrays your confidence, could you trust that person again?
3. Can you live with someone and yet not know who that person really is inside? Are you in that situation now?

Resource Reading
John 1

Part VI

Balancing Marriage with the Demands of Life

"When I walk on the beach to watch the sunset, I do not call out, 'A little more orange over to the right, please,' or 'Would you mind giving us less purple in the back?' No, I enjoy the always-different sunsets as they are. We do well to do the same with people we love."[32]

—Carl Rogers

How Men Get in the Doghouse[33]

"Husbands, love your wives, just as Christ loved the church and gave himself up for her to make her holy, cleansing her by the washing with water through the word." (Ephesians 5:25-26)

Some call it "Le Chateau Bow-wow!" which is a fancy name for the doghouse. Of course, when you're in the doghouse, a fancy title doesn't make it any less annoying. There's something strange about it, too: it is almost always *men* who are in the doghouse. The following are seven things which men are prone to do which will put them in "Le Chateau Bow-wow" for sure.

Mistake #1: Forget special events such as birthdays, anniversaries and Valentine's Day. To be forewarned is to be forearmed. Men and women are different—from their brains to their feet. Specials days mean far more to women than to men, so if you love someone special, men, you had better remember those special days.

Mistake #2: Admit that another woman is prettier than your wife or girlfriend. For instance: a pretty girl is walking down the street toward you. You notice that she is pretty, but you had better not notice for too long and it would definitely behoove you not to mention your observation to your wife or girlfriend. You see, your wife will be watching to see if you are watching. Once you have noticed that a pretty girl is there, it is best to pretend that she is invisible. Uh-huh. Like David of old, a second look is bound to get you into the doghouse—and fast.

Mistake #3: Buy your wife or girlfriend a dress that is two sizes too big. Better to err on the side of too small than for her to think that you think she wears a size fourteen when she really wears a size ten. Take it from me, men, your wives or girlfriends don't think the same way you do. When you go to the store and buy a board a foot too long, it's no big deal. You take a saw and whack off a foot or so. But when you get your wife a dress that's way too big, it is patently offensive. It's the doghouse for you for sure.

M*en and women are different—
from their brains to their feet.*

Mistake #4: Hesitate just the slightest in answering the question, "Do you think that I'm fat?" That will do it every time. You don't have to actually say so—just hesitate and you're in the doghouse. In some places in the world—especially where food is in short supply—it's a measure of success to be . . . well, not to be skinny, anyway. I remember one time seeing an old friend in Asia, and she said, "Oh, Dr. Sala, you look so nice and plump!" At first, I thought, "Thanks a lot!" and then I remembered that the comment was intended as a compliment.

For most women, however, there is a fixation with being overweight. Love her as she is. Life has a way of rearranging the corpuscles, and to expect her at age forty to look as she did at age twenty-five is un-realistic. Besides, you don't measure up to that standard either.

Mistake #5: Give your wife or girlfriend a small appliance such as a clock radio, an iron—that includes a curling iron—or any other thing that has a cord attached. Gifts like that just don't cut it. I learned that lesson the time I gave my wife a clock radio for Mother's Day. Actually, I thought I'd enjoy it at the same time. Take it from me—never again.

Insight

W*hen a husband really loves his wife (and she knows that she really is loved), his stay in the doghouse is very temporary. However, when she questions that she is loved, the man had better get comfortable in the doghouse, because it may take a while to get out.*

Mistake #6: After dinner, compliment her by saying, "That was a nice little dinner!" You'll end up in the doghouse for sure. What you meant to be a compliment will instead be taken as a backhanded insult.

Mistake #7: Asking, "How much did *that* thing cost?" In fact, any question along the lines where the implication is, "No matter what you paid for it, it wasn't worth it" is just a bad idea.

Men, as you well know, there are undoubtedly many other ways to get into the doghouse. Many of us are experts on getting into the doghouse, so in the next section, we'll learn how to get out.

Think on This

1. Are you like the fellow who said, "Why buy flowers? They just die!"? Part of our sexual difference is that

women appreciate flowers (really, men!) and by buying them for our wives or girlfriends we are giving a nonverbal message that says, "I recognize that flowers are meaningful to you and what is meaningful to you is important to me. Enjoy!"

3. What have you done this past week to show appreciation for your spouse?

Resource Reading
Ephesians 5:25-33

How to Get Out of the Doghouse[34]

"If I speak in the tongues of men and of angels, but have not love, I am only a resounding gong or a clanging cymbal." (1 Corinthians 13:1)

A young wife was pouring out her heart to her mother, describing how her husband had forgotten her birthday. Annoyed, she said, "Men are good for just one thing!" "Yes," said her mother, adding, "And thank goodness we don't have to parallel park very often."

Interested in knowing *how to get out* of the doghouse? These keys can save you from big trouble.

Key #1: Make it a habit to remember. Make a list of birthdays, anniversaries and other important days and put them on your calendar. They may not be important to you but they are to the woman in your life. "Do you know what today is?" a wife asked her husband. "Oh, yes!" he exclaimed, not wanting to admit he didn't know. All day long he wracked his brain. "What is today?" He asked his secretary. He even called his mother. Nobody knew what was special. To be on the safe side, he bought flowers from the florist and took her out for dinner. Still not sure what they were celebrating, as they climbed into bed, he asked, "Well, did today live up to your expectations?" "What do you mean?" she asked. "Well, remember, you asked me this morning if I knew what day this was?" "Oh that!" she exclaimed, adding, "I just couldn't remember the date—that's all!"

Key #2: Demonstrate your love—don't just say it. Talk is cheap. Diamonds are not. But, if diamonds are out of your price range, candy and flowers will definitely fit the bill. They make a statement that you remembered and went out of your way to say, "I love you." In his book *Love Languages* Dr. Gary Chapman contends that different people have different love languages. He believes there are five basic ways people express their love: 1) by saying it; 2) through gifts; 3) by touching someone physically; 4) by acts of service (fixing the dripping faucet, taking out the garbage, putting up the light in the sewing closet, doing something without being asked); and 5) by spending quality time together.[35]

B*eing open and vulnerable melts the ice and helps dissipate misunderstanding.*

We must remember when considering the demonstration of our love that it is a decision, a commitment to care, and that demonstrating it goes far beyond a Valentine's Day card or a box of candy.

Key #3: Do something special. Like what? Try breakfast in bed. Volunteer to baby-sit while your wife goes shopping. Arrange to go to the dentist with her instead of saying, "There's nothing to be afraid of. That little shot won't hurt much, and then you can't feel it when he takes out your tooth." Try asking her what she would like to watch on TV, even if it means you don't see the game you wanted to watch. Recognize she is a person with feelings, emotions and desires.

Key #4: Admit your mistakes and failures. "Before we married my husband was 'Mr. Right,' " said one young woman. "Then after we married, he was 'Mr. Always Right!' " Let's face it, men. We may know more about mechan-

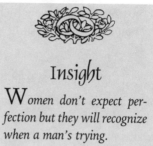

Insight

W*omen don't expect perfection but they will recognize when a man's trying.*

ical things than our wives. We may understand computers better. But if we balance that against what our wives know that we don't know, I have a feeling that we're not going to come out on top. So it just makes sense that we need to get good at saying, "I was wrong. Please forgive me!" with sincerity and genuineness. I can almost guarantee it will open the doghouse door.

Key #5: Try to listen, understand and then communicate. Being open and vulnerable melts the ice and helps dissipate misunderstanding.

Key #6: Lead the way spiritually. Praying together, reading the Bible together and going to church together build strong relationships.

Frankly, there are a lot more ways of getting *into* the doghouse than getting *out* of it, but believe me, nothing succeeds like sincerity, honesty, openness and being vulnerable. And don't forget the roses.

Think on This

1. Do you know when your wife's birthday is? Still remember your anniversary?

2. What is your wife's primary love language? What is yours?
3. What does your husband or wife do for you which is an expression of love which you really appreciate? Have you ever told him or her?

Resource Reading
1 Corinthians 13

Balancing Business and Family

*"Anyone, then, who knows the good he ought to
do and doesn't do it, sins." (James 4:17)*

How do you balance business with family commitments? How do you respond when your
child says, "Dad, how come you can never come to my
game? All the other kids' dads are there"? So you stutter
and stammer about how you can't get off work and that
you are overloaded and so forth, but your child simply
knows *you are not there.*

Stephen Carter is a Yale University law professor, and he
believes that ethical decisions boil down to one question,
"What do you really value?" He believes the issue of
whether or not you take time to be at your son's game or
your daughter's school presentation is a values-related decision. He says that likewise the father who tells his son he
will be at the school play and doesn't show up, is, by his actions, telling his son what he really values. The answer, he
believes, is not to make promises that are likely to be broken and to include your kids' activities in your priority
list.[36]

Dennis Rainey faced that same situation when his work required him to be away from home for a speaking engagement at the same time his daughter became a homecoming queen candidate at her high school. Naturally, she wanted her dad there for the big occasion. After all, on-the-road speaking engagements for Dennis Rainey were as common as sunrise and sunset—well, almost—but his daughter's becoming homecoming queen was a once-in-a-lifetime experience.

Rainey believes that there are four steps to balancing family commitment with work-related responsibilities. First, pray about the situation. Second, set priorities. Third, be willing to pay the price, and fourth, have a plan.[37]

W*hen you are confronted with tough decisions: pray, prioritize, pay the price and formulate a plan.*

In praying about the situation you have to remind yourself that nothing comes as a surprise to God. Before your child was ever conceived, God knew that the day would come when your big presentation at work would fall on the opening day of the baseball season. "God loves the prayer of the helpless parent," says Rainey. "When you ask Him for wisdom, you switch gears and also say, 'Lord, Your value system is different from mine. What's important in this situation?' "

Then you set priorities. Which is more important? The relationship you have with your child or avoiding moving the presentation to another date?

The third consideration is what price is attached to your decision, no matter what it is? Negotiation and compromise are all part of the strategy of conflict resolution, so you ask, "How can I handle this and keep everyone happy?" or "Am I willing to pay the price if I come down on one side or the other of this issue?" You need to realize right off the bat that you probably can't keep everyone happy. Bill Cosby once said that he did not know the secret of success but he did know that the formula for failure is trying to keep all of the people happy all of the time.

Insight

While most men say that their families come before their work, the amount of time given to each often makes that statement unconvincing.

Finally, you must forge a plan. For Dennis Rainey, the plan included his personally paying the costs of reprinting tickets to the event at which he was to speak, moving it to another night and attending the prom his daughter felt was important. And did this make everyone happy? Not necessarily, but it made his daughter supremely happy. His doing what he did made a statement as far as his daughter is concerned, and she will never forget it.

A final thought. When you come to the end of your life, I doubt that God will ask you about how many presentations you made, but He will ask you about how good a parent you were—of that I am quite certain. In summary, when you are confronted with tough decisions: pray, prioritize, pay the price and formulate a plan. Someday you will be glad—very glad—that you did.

Think on This

1. Have you had a conflict between work and a commitment you made to your wife and/or kids? How did you resolve this?

2. Ten years from now you will not remember whether or not you worked overtime, but your youngster will remember whether you were at opening day for the Little League baseball season. Try to avoid some scheduling problems by getting a calendar and marking it with commitments to your family before you fill up the schedule with other things.

3. If you find it hard to say, "No," learn to say, "I'd like to say, 'Yes,' but I can't because I've made a previous commitment for that day." (Telling the other person what it is you will be doing is neither important nor any of their business!). Try it! It works. I've been doing it for years. Besides, it sounds very businesslike and official.

Resource Reading
2 Samuel 12

Tђe Cost of a Seconð Salary

"Whatever you do, work at it with all your heart, as working for the Lord, not for men." (Colossians 3:23)

How do husbands and wives feel about working wives and mothers? That was the question that I posed on one of my radio programs, asking people to respond and to register their thoughts. Almost as many men as women responded, which came as some surprise to me.

One husband wrote, "Both of us must work. My salary only meets sixty-two percent of our needs. We have one car, usually in need of repair. It goes without saying what a hassle life can be like this. My job doesn't allow time for me to look for another one. Our biggest need: time together as a family and as a husband and a wife."

Another said, "My wife just quit work after almost twenty years of holding down a very good job. In analyzing our income, we discovered that by the time we paid for transportation, clothes, lunches, etc., etc., that the actual amount which she netted was only five percent of her salary, and we said, 'It's just not worth it.' "

Some wives were quick to point out that they were pulling an equal share of the load outside the home, but when it came to domestic tasks, there was no equality. The responsibility of the home was theirs alone. One woman wrote, "I am employed as a secretary, full time, and have worked all my life—have been married thirty-five years and reared one daughter. I try so hard to do everything right at home: do my work, cook meals and all those things a wife does. I have a husband who comes home from work, and usually there is never a word said except to gripe about this or that not being done, or done his way. Honestly, I would give anything to be greeted with a smile—just a smile—and it would be nice for him to add, 'How was your day?' "

Y*our children are the loan of a life—*
not a permanent possession or
an interruption of your career.

A retired mother of six adult children, now in her seventies, wrote, "My one wish was to be at home [with my children]. I worked thirty years and raised the family. My husband is a farmer and there was never enough." Then somewhat nostalgically she wrote, "You do miss something [when working] that never comes back."

Can a mother work, holding down a responsible position and still have time for her children? Before you answer, you need to hear what one woman wrote. "I have been working in the insurance field since I was sixteen and have only stayed home to have my boys, six weeks at a time—then back to work. I am now age forty-seven and

president of five corpora-
tions, as well as a trustee
of the holding company. I
have great responsibility
on my shoulders, but I can
honestly tell you that my
greatest and always my
most joyous responsibility
has been my husband and
children. God first, family
next and then career has

Insight

Choosing to work or be at home has to include the intangibles as well as how much additional income a second salary provides.

always been my motto and the only one that will work. I
am so proud of my family and feel totally fulfilled because
I have always put them as the most important. I wish that
women everywhere would cherish the moments they
have with their 'borrowed children.' There is nothing—I
mean nothing—in the business world that has ever come
close to the fulfillment children and family bring."

The final paragraph written by this remarkable woman
read, "I would love to tell [mothers who can stay at
home] how lucky they are to stay home and enjoy every
minute with their growing children."

And there you have it—different responses to the issue
of the importance of income from a working wife and
mother and what priority she gives to her children and family.

Obviously it is an issue which has to be decided on a
number of factors, including the age of the children, the
importance of income and the support a husband and father gives in the process.

But there is one thing for sure: Your children are the
loan of a life—not a permanent possession or an interruption of your career. They are possibilities for better or for

worse, opportunities which are never to be repeated. Think about it.

Think on This

When you consider the issue of working outside the home versus being a stay-at-home mom, try to see the whole picture, looking beyond the additional income which a full-time job would provide. As you think and pray about the issue, take a sheet of paper, draw a line down the center and write down the options for each choice and the immediate as well as long-range consequences you see from each choice. As you ponder this, pray, "Lord, You know our hearts as well as our needs. Please speak to our hearts and make Your will very clear. Show us Your will." He will. Remember, Jesus promised that those who follow Him would never walk in darkness (see John 8:12).

Resource Reading
Psalm 127

Myths That Can Wreck Your Marriage

"[Love] is not rude, it is not self-seeking, it is not easily angered, it keeps no record of wrongs. Love does not delight in evil but rejoices with the truth. It always protects, always trusts, always hopes, always perseveres.

Love never fails." (1 Corinthians 13:5-8)

Both men and women struggle with an abysmal ignorance of each other's psychological makeup. We subsequently live with myths and misconceptions that seem to be passed from generation to generation. Consider the following:

Myth #1: "If he really loved me, he'd know what I want!" This is not exclusively a woman's myth. Both husbands and wives at times find difficulty in expressing what is really on their hearts, and no matter how much love there is in a relationship, there has to be communication to express the feelings of a heart. Neither men nor women are mind readers, so actual verbal communication is vital to the health of a relationship.

Myth #2: The quality of the time we spend together as a family is more important than the quantity of time we spend together. Put this one to rest once and for all. There is no way you can substitute being together, feeling what the other feels, experiencing all the flavors and variations of life and love without actually being together. Having an hour or two with your child on the weekend is no substitute for just being there: putting him to bed, reading to him, showing an interest in the things that are going on in his life.

Your physical presence is an expression of love which cannot be substituted with brief appearances labeled "quality time." A survey of 3,000 couples who consider their marriages to be "strong" and "close" say they spend "a great deal of time together." As one woman with thirty years of marriage behind her put it, "Heartfelt conversations simply cannot be squeezed into little snatches of time."

Y*our physical presence is an expression of love which cannot be substituted with brief appearances labeled "quality time."*

Myth #3: Having a baby will bring us together. Wrong again! The fact is that having a youngster can produce a considerable amount of stress in a marriage. While it can be an enriching experience, feeding schedules, crying babies and interruptions in your schedule are generally not conducive to drawing you closer to each other. Example: who is responsible to get the bottle for the baby when both of you are tired and it's 3 a.m. on Sunday morning? Uh-huh! Split decision on that already.

Myth #4: Times of crisis make a marriage stronger.
While that can well be true, it generally works the other
way. A crisis in life—whether it is personal, financial or a
family crisis involving parents or relatives—can do one of
two things: it can draw you closer to each other or it can
push you farther apart.

Your relationship with
the Lord and your ability to
see the hand of God in what
happens also has a signifi-
cant role in crisis situations. If you have a healthy
relationship with the Lord,
difficulty can bring you
closer to both Him and
your spouse. But if you do
not have a right relation-

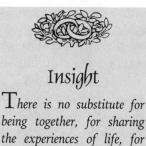

Insight

There is no substitute for
being together, for sharing
the experiences of life, for
feeling what the other feels.

ship with God, difficulties can come between you as you
play the blame game, accusing your spouse of being the
reason for trouble.

**Myth #5: My personal happiness is the most impor-
tant thing in my life.** I label this as a myth based upon the
fact that happiness is dependent on far more than circumstances. Clearly, changing partners and circumstances
doesn't bring happiness when you take misery with you.
The fact is that misery begets misery, and changing partners or circumstances usually only compounds the difficulty. Presently more than half of all marriages end in
failure, and of that number seventy-five percent will try
again, and of that number sixty percent fail.[38]

George Barna says, "Born-again Christians are slightly
more likely than non-Christians to go through a divorce,
with 26% of born-agains and 22% of non-Christians having gone through a divorce some time in their life." [39] This

can be explained by the too-common attitude among Christians that "Surely God doesn't want me to be unhappy, so if my spouse can't make me happy, surely He wouldn't want me to stay in this marriage." The solution is to not run from problems, but to solve them with God's help and your patient persistence. Joy, not happiness, is the great reward of having done the right thing, overcoming the difficulties that could sink the ship of your marriage. Solving problems is not easy. But tough as it is, it's the only way to real fulfillment.

Think on This

1. Being the right person is far more important than striving to make the other person the "right person." Giving allowance to your mate to be less than perfect also creates room for your humanity as well.
2. Why do you think individuals in second marriages have an even greater rate of failure than those in first-time marriages?

Resource Reading
1 Corinthians 13:5-13

Money Can Wreck Your Marriage

"For the love of money is a root of all kinds of evil. Some people, eager for money, have wandered from the faith and pierced themselves with many griefs." (1 Timothy 6:10)

Jack and his wife Sue should have more than enough to be satisfied. He's an attorney with a six-figure income and a growing practice; she's an interior decorator. In the early years of their marriage they often talked for hours at a time and when words were exhausted, they would hold hands, communicating with their hearts.

Now, they are hopelessly in debt, communication is strained and each blames the other for their problems. "All you ever do is work, work, work!" she yells. He answers, "I'm only trying to earn enough money to satisfy you!"

Surprising as it may be to some, money disagreements destroy more marriages than do affairs! In at least eighty-five percent of all broken homes, how money is handled is a major source of disagreement.

Is money management ruining your marriage? The issue is not how much you have or how little you have. It's what you do with what you do have! Whoever controls the spending has power and the battle for control is really a power issue.

If money is producing conflict in your marriage, apply the following guidelines:

Guideline #1: Stop using money as a weapon to hurt each other. Credit card transactions can become "an eye-for-an-eye," with each additional purchase more ammunition in a mounting battle. This kind of fighting and retaliation only results in both of you becoming blind and eventually broke. It is kind of like trying to stop a sinking ship by punching a hole in the hull—it just doesn't work. You need to ask yourself, "Is it worth it to let money destroy our relationship?"

Y*ou made a commitment to each other at the marriage altar and money is just as much part of that commitment as is sexual fidelity.*

Guideline #2: Stop fighting and start talking. The first positive step toward fixing the damage to your relationship is to get a budget—and don't be like the fellow who swore that he would live within his budget even if it meant borrowing money to do it. Agree that you will not make any major purchases without both of you consenting to them. You made a commitment to each other at the marriage altar and money is just as much part of that commitment as is sexual fidelity.

Guideline #3: Start paying cash. If you don't have it, don't spend it. This one is not only common sense but it is also in keeping with a scriptural principle. "Let no debt remain outstanding, except the continuing debt to love one another," wrote Paul in Romans 13:8. Eliminating the interest that is probably killing you can increase your buying power by at least forty percent. Perform plastic surgery on those credit cards: cut them up! When the cash runs out, stop spending until the next paycheck.

Guideline #4: Analyze your need to spend what you don't have. In some cases, people spend money to impress people whom they don't like. But when you spend what you don't have to impress someone you don't even like, you are only hurting yourself. Others spend money they don't have in an attempt to demonstrate love. For yet others, spending money is a high almost akin to an addiction. Yet—and this is where the danger becomes

Insight

Since there are only three things you can do with money—save it, give it away or spend it—you wouldn't think it would be the major problem in marriage that it is. Money represents power and power creates a pecking order, and in this lies the problem.

evident—abuse of your contract with each other does about as much to destroy intimacy as forfeiting a shower for a month or two. It drives a hard and fast wedge between you.

Guideline #5: Get help. You can start over but you never start again. But starting over—with the one who stood by your side and said, "I do!"—can result in rebuilding your marriage, the intimacy you once enjoyed and eventually your financial nest egg.

Guideline #6: Ask each other's forgiveness and seek God's help. Long ago Scripture said that a threefold cord cannot be broken (see Ecclesiastes 4:12), and when two are willing to say, "Lord, we need Your help; this is too big for us," it is amazing how quickly the fighting stops and the building begins.

Life is too short to have your home broken up by poor money management. It just isn't worth it. Jesus was right when he said, "a man's life does not consist in the abundance of his possessions" (Luke 12:15). It's still true.

Think on This

1. Begin with a budget. Start by writing down everything you spend. You may be surprised.
2. Understand that God blesses you when you honor Him by refusing to violate scriptural principles such as Romans 13:8, which basically says, "Owe no man anything but to love one another."
3. Have you made it a practice to give God a tenth (the Bible calls it a tithe) of what you have? (See Malachi 3:10 and 1 Corinthians 16:2.) If you adopt this practice, you will soon discover the amazing truth that the nine-tenths left over goes farther than the entire original sum ever did.

Resource Reading
2 Corinthians 8

For Better,
For Worse

"Guard yourself in your spirit, and do not break faith with the wife of your youth." (Malachi 2:15)

Do you remember those words, "for better, for worse, for richer, for poorer, in sickness and in health, 'til death us do part?" They are part of the Episcopal wedding ceremony—the one that you traditionally hear at weddings. Are they well-meaning platitudes which are impossible to keep? Or is such commitment—to death—a possibility even today?

It has been said that most marriages begin with both partners trusting each other, believing that they will never hurt each other, that nothing will ever infringe on their perfect happiness. They have faith that their marriage will endure tests and trials and that they will come out victors with their marriage, and all its inherent intimacy and trust, intact. The first breaking of that faith is not the first act of extramarital intercourse, it is that moment when one of the partners looks outside the marriage relationship in search of intimacy or fulfillment, and keeps that decision a secret. That is the true betrayal of trust.

What's your verdict? When does a person break faith with his mate? Does a husband break faith with his wife when he confides in his secretary over lunch and talks with her about intimate details of his life—details which he hesitates to share with his wife? Does a wife break faith with her husband when she acknowledges compliments from male admirers in such a way that she sends nonverbal messages that say, "I like the attention you are giving to me"? Does a person break faith with a mate when he or she begins to withhold part of the truth? "White lies" is the expression we often use to justify bending the truth.

Infidelity starts when we begin to flirt with the idea that we are unnoticed or taken for granted. The second step is nourishing a fantasy or a relationship which begins to develop with another person. It's fed by deceit, covering your tracks, making phone calls which you would prefer your mate not know about, arranging your schedule so that you have casual contact with another person whose company you enjoy.

Keeping faith is more than a discipline.
It's the key to keeping love vibrant and alive.

At first, it is not that another has taken the place which your mate has in your life. It's that your ego has dislodged the priority which the other had in your heart. Love demands that your mate comes first, but selfishness insists that your happiness and fulfillment come before commitment or loyalty. The conflict produces what psychologists call "a double bind." Trapped by deceit, you live one kind of a life but covertly nourish another, even if it is "only" a fantasy life.

When you begin to feel that you are being taken for granted, it is easy to justify allowing your heart to stray. "He never notices what I do for him!" "If he would only tell me that he loves me!" "She's the problem in our home." How quickly we point the finger of responsibility at the other and say, "It's not my fault." Something new? No! Something very old. Adam, our first father, tried to avoid responsibility for his failure as he pointed to Eve and said, "She took of the fruit and I did eat it" (see Genesis 3:12).

Insight

Before an individual is ever unfaithful to his or her spouse, he or she commits emotional infidelity—the little lies, the small scenarios of deceit and the insincere words and comments which are made.

You may be asking, "OK, what do I do when we begin to break faith with each other?" First, recognize how deadly the whole issue is when you catch yourself beginning the process of rationalization or feeling sorry for yourself, taken for granted or neglected. Second, address the issue by confronting your mate and expressing the feelings which are troubling you. Third, begin to build on the positive. This may require help or counseling. It may mean you learn how to communicate or become willing to be vulnerable. You begin to recognize that your marriage has lost its sparkle and has reached a stalemate.

Breaking faith with each other begins in the mind, but ultimately it is played out in terms of broken relationships and broken hearts. Keeping faith is more than a discipline. It's the key to keeping love vibrant and alive.

Think on This

1. Take time to thoughtfully review the three guidelines listed on the previous page and pray, asking God to show you what you need to do in your own marriage.
2. Have you honestly kept faith with your mate? Is there something you need to talk about? Remember you can choose the time and the place and the way you present your concern.

Resource Reading
Hosea 1–2

Part VII

Touching God for Your Marriage

"You can do more than pray after you've prayed, but you cannot do more than pray until you have prayed."[40]

—John Bunyan

Day 44

Can This Marriage Be Saved?

"I have loved you with an everlasting love;
I have drawn you with loving-kindness.
I will build you up again,
. . . O Virgin Israel." (Jeremiah 31:3-4)

A husband and a wife come together in marriage
and celebrate their love. Nine months later a son
is born. They name him Jezreel but call him Jesse for
short. Some people think that having children will bring
them closer together, but in many cases children put
stress on a marriage. That's what happened with this couple. The husband was preoccupied with his work and he
and his wife began to drift.

Eventually a second child was born—a little girl with
dark eyes and the features of her mother. But things between the couple were no better. The relationship was
strained, communication was difficult and intimacy was
gone.

Then what the husband had suspected in his darkest
moments becomes evident. His wife is seeing another
man. He's sure this time because she is pregnant and he

knows he is not the father of the child. Now, he faces the most difficult decision of his life. Should he tell her, "Get out; you have betrayed my trust, you have darkened my name, you are not fit to be my wife"? He thought about it, that's for sure; but instead, for whatever reasons, he chose to stand by her. And though it was not easy, he decided to be a father to the unborn child whom he called "Lo-Ammi," which in Hebrew literally means, "Not mine!"

After the baby was born, the wife, Gomer, was gone more and more. Some nights she didn't come home at all. Can you imagine how Hosea must have felt, answering the tough questions his children posed? As the older children knelt to say their prayers at night they asked, "Daddy, where's Mommy? When is she coming home?"

The story which I have just related is as current as the tabloid on the newsstand or the soap opera on television, but actually it took place over 2,000 years ago. You can read about it in the Old Testament book of Hosea.

M*arriage burnout is a condition which exists when a marriage suffers from stress, busyness and wrong priorities.*

Broken homes, broken promises and broken hearts are not new. They are as old as human nature itself. If Hosea and Gomer were alive today we might well describe their marriage as one suffering from burnout, a twenty-first century term used to describe a centuries-old problem.

Marriage burnout is a condition which exists when a marriage suffers from stress, busyness and wrong priorities. In chess when you are confronted with a stalemate, you just can't move, but in marriage when you have a stalemate, you are in big trouble. Burnout is a prelude to the devastating consequences of a broken home and broken hearts.

When the fire goes out of romance, can anything be done? In the story which I related, Hosea kept his marriage together by a gargantuan effort on his part to reconcile and to bend in humility.

Long ago, God gave the Ephesians a formula to restore their love for Him (see Revelation 2:4-7). The same three words apply to a marriage which has grown cold and mechanical. Those three words are 1) REMEMBER, 2) REPENT, 3) RETURN. Why not first repent, then remember and return? When our love grows cold and our hearts grow hard, we need to re-

Insight

Marriage burnout doesn't have to be fatal, but the symptoms of boredom, indifference and disinterest are red flags that demand you take steps to reverse the inevitable slide toward a broken home.

member in order to let our emotions remind us of what things used to be and what they can be again. Repenting means changing our minds, overcoming the stubbornness which contributed to the problem and finally returning to the way we once lived.

Have I described your marriage today? A coldness has chilled your home. Things are mechanical and perfunctory. You respond out of duty or obligation, not passion and feeling. Ask God to touch your hearts. Grasp hands together and pray for a renewal. Remembering, repenting and returning are still the answer to marriage burnout.

Think on This

1. Remember. Make a list of five outstanding things you did together in the early days of your courtship or marriage. Are those things still happening? Why not?
2. Repent. That's making a definite decision to completely change the direction your marriage is headed. Yes, it's worth it. Build on those great memories and years.
3. Return. That means go back to the place where you got off track and renew your love and commitment to each other.

Resource Reading
Jeremiah 31

God's Plan
for Your Marriage

*"Do two walk together unless they have agreed
to do so?" (Amos 3:3)*

D oing Without Marriage" was the caption of an
article that described what is happening to families in Europe.[41] Years ago the Netherlands was a staunch
Christian nation where John Calvin's theology was
closely followed. But today the great churches are empty,
prostitution is legal, drugs are available in boutiques, and
marriage—traditional marriage between a male and a female—is something that happens less and less.

In Scandinavian countries it is not only socially acceptable to live together without being married, but legal and
so common that the majority of children born in Sweden,
Norway and Denmark are born to unmarried mothers.[42]

What has happened in the past generation to reverse
time-honored traditions? There are a number of answers
to that question but by and large what has happened to
the family and to its traditional values has been the result
of the rejection of the biblical plan for the family. And the

farther we move away from God's blueprint the more unstable the family unit.

Many feminists reject the biblical formula, understanding neither the purpose of God's direction nor the relationship He intends between a husband and a wife. Many women believe that male leadership is domination and want their freedom. But God's intention was never to enslave women or to make them inferior to their husbands.

As Gary Chapman pointed out, " . . . the man and his wife were instructed to subdue the earth and to rule over the fish of the sea, the birds of the air, and other living creatures. The man was not instructed to subdue his wife. He was told to become 'one flesh' with her."[43] God's purpose was a partnership, a oneness which allows for individuality and differences but still affirms the oneness of a marriage and family.

> T*he farther we move away from God's blueprint the more unstable the family unit.*

It has been interesting to me to note that God's plan is universal and all-comprehensive. It spans cultures, centuries and differences in economic and educational backgrounds. God never gave one plan for Europeans, another for Asians and another for the rest of the world. He made us, and as Architect and Builder, He also knows how we can find personal happiness and how our children can find security and meaning in life.

Feminists are not the only ones who misunderstand the relationship which God intended in marriage. Vast numbers of people, including those who go to church each Sunday, never get it either. Five times in the Bible God stresses that a husband and wife are to be one, and the analogy of the human body—a unit with a diversity of functions—helps illustrate this truth. You have two hands which function independently yet work together in harmony to catch a ball, to fix a meal, to hold a baby. Yes, you can do those tasks with one hand, but two hands work-

Insight

God's intention was that husbands and wives should be a team, with each fulfilling his or her own unique role in life.

ing together in harmony make everything easier and more efficient.

Charlie Shedd said that God's purpose for husbands was like that of the conductor of an orchestra, who brings harmony to all the members. I like what Ambrose Bierce wrote about marriage: "Marriage is a community consisting of a master, a mistress, and two slaves, making in all, two."[44]

Frankly, it isn't just in Amsterdam or Oslo where people are in need of returning to the biblical pattern. It's Manila, Hong Kong, Xiamen, Berlin and where you live as well.

When we disregard God's blueprint for us we're on our own and, let's face it, we've failed miserably trying to reinvent the formula. It's time to understand God's purpose and plan, for only then will the family come together again.

Think on This

1. There is a correlation between the distance we have come from God's purpose and the instability of life. Why is that? Is it just as true of individuals as it is of society?
2. It is a fact that alternative lifestyles just don't work; however, they have become part of our culture today.

If your youngster came home from school and said, "Billy has two daddies at home but no mommy," how would you handle this?

3. How would you explain the fact that you can accept individuals for who they are but cannot endorse their lifestyle?

Resource Reading
Genesis 1

Bringing Your Mate to Christ

"Wives, in the same way be submissive to your husbands so that, if any of them do not believe the word, they may be won over without words by the behavior of their wives, when they see the purity and reverence of your lives." (1 Peter 3:1-2)

Dear Dr. Sala," writes a friend of *Guidelines*, "my two daughters and I have been praying for my husband to accept salvation for three years now. We do hope that this prayer will be answered in God's good timing. Please pray that we'll not grow weary and will continue to pray for him."

That plea is typical of the many letters which come to us at *Guidelines*. Usually it is women who ask us to pray for husbands, but sometimes it is the husband who says, "My wife decided she doesn't want to be married anymore and walked out on us." In those cases, it is a brokenhearted husband who has lost his wife and the mother of his children that writes to us, asking us to share his pain and pray that their marriage might be repaired.

We live in an imperfect, broken world, but does this mean we simply have to accept the fact that this is the way it is, or can prayer change situations?

First, a word of comfort. There are always going to be times when we don't know how to pray, but we can take heart in what Paul wrote to the Romans—that the Spirit Himself makes intercession for us because we don't know how to pray as we ought (see Romans 8:26). But when we are praying for a husband or wife, son or daughter to come to a saving knowledge of Jesus Christ, the words will just flow. You can pray with confidence because God's Word has made it crystal clear that it is His will for the one you love to find His Son.

"Please pray for my husband that he may come to Christ, if this is God's will," a woman once asked of me. Without much comment I took my Bible and read from Second Peter 3:9, which says, "The Lord is not slow in keeping his promise, as some understand slowness. He is patient with you, not wanting anyone to perish, but everyone to come to repentance." "Does *everyone* include your husband?" I asked. Issue concluded.

Y*ou can pray with confidence because God's Word has made it crystal clear that it is His will for the one you love to find His Son.*

Praying expectantly and with confidence is important. "My wife is not a Christian," men sometimes say. "Do you believe God will honor your prayers and bring her to Himself?" I ask. "Yes," men generally say. I tell them, "Then you should say, 'My wife is *not yet* a Christian.' "

In his first letter, Peter—a man's man if there ever was one—says that how a woman lives is a message which communicates to her husband something like this: "You see the difference God has made in my life. The change in how I treat you is evidence that something real, something meaningful has happened to me" (see 1 Peter 3:1-2).

Sometimes the best thing that a woman can do to help bring her husband to Christ is to stay home some and be a companion and friend to her mate. "You mean stay home instead of going to church?" Sometimes. One frustrated husband told his wife, "You might as well live with your Jesus because you're never at home

Insight

It is a wonderful thing to realize that when you pray for your husband or wife to come to Christ you are praying in the will of God (see 1 John 5:14).

anymore." He didn't like that she was gone several nights a week as well as on Sundays.

Scores of individuals—both husbands and wives—having seen a tremendous change for the better in the one they married, will sit up and take notice that something important has happened in their spouse's life and will begin to follow Jesus Christ as a result.

There comes a time when you can share your faith openly with love and concern. It's easy. The work has already been done. The Holy Spirit has prepared the person and all you need to say is, "This is the way to the foot of the cross. Let's go together." God has a timetable and wise is the one who reads the signals and knows when to say, "It's time to get on board. Let's go as a family."

Think on This

1. In the Scripture reference at the beginning of this selection, Peter talks about husbands being "won over without words by the behavior of their wives." What tangible evidence of a changed life and disposition do men look for?

2. In his book *The Case for Christ* Lee Strobel tells how the changes he saw in his wife following her conversion caused him as a skeptic to take a hard look at Jesus Christ and eventually resulted in his conversion.

3. There are seasons to life and times when our hearts are searching. Rest with confident assurance that your mate will come to Christ. Look for the opening and be ready to show your husband or wife how simple it is to become a believer.

4. Pray, asking the Lord to help you to be sensitive regarding timing, then be prepared when you sense that time has come.

Resource Reading
1 Peter 3:1-6

Praying as a Couple

"Finally, all of you, live in harmony with one another; be sympathetic, love as brothers, be compassionate and humble. Do not repay evil with evil or insult with insult, but with blessing, because to this you were called so that you may inherit a blessing." (1 Peter 3:8-9)

So, you have never prayed with your husband or wife. Do you mind if I ask, "Why not?" More than a few times I have asked couples that question and I have gotten a wide variety of answers. I often get the feeling that people feel awkward or clumsy praying together. In some cases they think that prayer is a private matter or that it belongs in church, or they feel embarrassed to pray together. But once a couple learns what prayer can do for their relationship, they change and change quickly.

Prayer is conversation between you and your heavenly Father, it's just that simple. Don't forget that God already knows everything about you, everything that takes place between you and your mate—and between you and everybody else for that matter. There are no surprises with

Him. You've also got to remember that because you are a child of God He loves you far more than you could possibly fathom.

If you've never prayed together as a couple, I have a suggestion. Sit together at a table with an empty chair and think of prayer as a simple conversation between you and Jesus Christ. Talk to Him as though He were actually sitting there. By the way, hold hands when you pray. There's something about touching each other as you touch God that makes for powerful chemistry.

You can pray together at any time, but unless you pray together at a particular time of the day, you will probably not make prayer a habit.

Don't forget that God already knows everything about you, everything that takes place between you and your mate—and between you and everybody else for that matter.

For many years my wife and I have made our time of prayer the first thing in the morning. I'll often stagger downstairs, make a pot of coffee, and by then Darlene manages to join me. We will often drink coffee together and pray, one voicing thoughts in simple, not-very-long-phrases, then the other.

What can prayer do for a couple? Plenty! It can open the door for effective communication, help you to address issues that could tear you apart, help you to find God's power in your personal lives in ways that you would never discover otherwise, give you wisdom in knowing how to parent, how to cope with the problems of work and how to stay on top of various circumstances in your lives.

Recently I was talking with a couple who have all but given up on their marriage. Four children from ages six to fourteen are involved. The father doesn't want a broken home. Neither do the children, but unless God does something, the marriage is go-

Insight

If God says "Pray about everything," then He intends to do something about everything!

ing to be history. "How long has it been since the two of you have prayed together?" I asked. They looked at each other and the husband said, "I don't know." Thinking for a moment the wife replied, "It's been at least four years."

For most of those years the couple has been in counseling. A lot of hours and more than a little money has gone into saving that marriage, but not once have they joined hands and said, "God, You know what is happening to our lives. We need Your help, Lord. Help us to be the people You want us to be, and forgive us for our sins and failures."

When a couple will agree to pray together—no matter what has happened, from infidelity to poor communication—the relationship will move toward a solution. But in closing I must warn you of something: there is danger involved in prayer. It can upset your agenda, but it can bring healing and hope for a better marriage. The danger is well worth facing.

Think on This

1. In the event that prayer is new to you, put an empty chair at your table and visualize Jesus Christ sitting there in person. Yes, I think He would have a cup of coffee with you. Should this happen, what would you

talk about? What needs would you tell Him about? That's what conversational prayer is, and I recommend it.

2. What is the best time for you and your mate to pray together? First thing in the morning? Last thing at night? Immediately after dinner? Set a time and try to make praying together a habit.

Resource Reading
1 Peter 3:1-12

Prayer Therapy and Marriage

"Our help is in the name of the LORD, the Maker of heaven and earth." (Psalm 124:8)

D oes prayer make a difference in a marriage? Sociologist Andrew M. Greeley believes it does. Surveys of married couples done in conjunction with the Gallup Poll and the National Opinion Research Center confirmed what Greeley already knew as a Catholic priest: When people pray together, they have a far greater chance of dealing with problems that can cause marriages to crash and burn. Prayer doesn't eliminate all the problems but it does give individuals a means of coping with them.

The surveys reveal that seventy-five percent of couples who pray together say their marriage is "very happy" compared to fifty-seven percent of those who never pray. Inversely, fifty-eight percent of those "who are not very religious," have serious marital problems compared with forty-five percent of those who describe themselves as religious. Greeley believes that prayer—rather than the frequency of sex in marriage—is the most accurate predictor of marital happiness.[45]

This news, of course, will cause hundreds of unhappy couples to start praying together every day, right? Probably not, though I wish that were true. Why don't we pray? Pride, stubbornness, possibly ignorance. There is, however, a powerful therapy to prayer when a couple will come together once every day, clasp hands and pray using simple, everyday language and terms, talking to God as though He were the third party of a conversation.

What does prayer do for a couple and what are the benefits of prayer therapy?

Benefit #1: Prayer reduces us to the same level. The issue of power—who is in charge—is one of the most frequent causes of marital battles. But when you pray you are on equal footing. It's somewhat humiliating, as well, because prayer forces us to recognize that God is sovereign and we are human. David cried out, "As a father has compassion on his children, so the LORD has compassion on those who fear him; . . . he remembers that we are dust" (Psalm 103:13-14).

P*rayer doesn't eliminate all the problems but it does give individuals a means of coping with them.*

Benefit #2: Prayer brings an arbitrator, a referee, to the table. Prayer can lower the emotional temperature of a relationship. Arguments are gradually diffused as you say, "Lord, we look at this issue differently. But we want Your will. What do You want us to do?"

Benefit #3: Prayer is the key to communication. You can pray standing up, sitting down, lying down or on your face before God. But when you pray with your mate, I suggest you join hands in an expression of oneness. It's hard to be angry when you vent your emotions openly and honestly before God. Prayer drains the bitterness from your heart, which then enables you to communicate, to talk about what really concerns you.

Insight

You *are a composite of the emotional, the physical and the spiritual, and prayer brings union to your spiritual nature which then trickles into every other area of your life.*

Benefit #4: Prayer therapy changes your heart and mellows your spirit. The benefit here is not saying words without meaning, but meaning what you say—which then gradually helps you to change your life.

Benefit #5: Prayer results in intimacy and sexual fulfillment which can happen no other way than through spiritual union. According to valid research it is a fact that the greater a couple's religious commitment, the more satisfying their sexual relationship.

Over the years I have challenged thousands of couples to put the entire issue to a thirty-day test. Agree together that for just thirty days you will take a few minutes every day and pray together. I am convinced that if you take the thirty-day test, you'll never stop.

Think on This

Take the thirty-day challenge and agree that you will pray together every day (if you have an early morning appointment and miss a day, don't quit), clasping hands and voicing your thoughts in simple phrases. If you cannot see a noticeable change in your relationship and peace of mind, forget it, but I can assure you that if you really take this seriously, you'll never quit.

Resource Reading
Psalm 124

Part VIII

Building for Tomorrow

"Marriage is a life work which some scarcely begin and only a minor few ever fully achieve."[46]

—Vernon Grounds

The Chemistry of Love

"Husbands, love your wives, just as Christ loved the church." (Ephesians 5:25)

In my resource file are a variety of folders which are filed alphabetically by subject. Thinking of today's selection, I happened to notice that the file captioned "LOVE" is nestled between the one captioned "LONELINESS" and the one on "MARRIAGE." That is pretty true to life: love is what it takes to turn loneliness to marriage.

Is love only a Western idea, a romantic notion which came from Europe and is embraced by only segments of civilization? Or is love a universal emotion, a deep-seated response of the heart which can sometimes cause emotion to prevail over reason?

For a long time anthropologists felt that love was a romantic concept which came from Europe and that it was not applicable to all civilizations the world over. That notion, however, is being debunked with solid scientific research which says love is a universal commodity, the glue which holds relationships together whether the marriage is arranged to keep family fortunes together, or a result of boy meeting girl.

An extensive research project took place in some 166 different cultures in almost as many countries and the findings of that research indicate that romantic love is prevalent in at least 147 of the 166 cultures. In the nineteen where it was not detected, authors of the study, William Jankowiak and Edward Fisher, say that the lack "probably reflects a deficiency of their study methods, not of local ardor."[47] Interesting!

Chalk another one up for scientific research! Scientists have just confirmed what parents have known for centuries: When the spark of love ignites in the breast of a young person, life will never be the same.

L*ove is God's answer to the loneliness of the human heart and the door to meaningful relationships.*

Another finding of the study indicated that in polygamous cultures, where a husband has more than one wife, there was almost always one wife who was special, one whom he really loved. For example, among the polygamous farmers of Kenya, "a man almost always married first for practical reasons. If he could afford more wives, he might then marry for romance." One eighty-year-old Kenyan spoke warmly of wife number four: "She was the wife of my heart. . . . I could look at her and she at me, no words would pass, just a smile."[48]

It is that look, that smile, that almost indescribable something that makes the chemistry of love what it is. The world's oldest textbook on marriage, the Bible, talks a great deal of love and its place in the relationship of a husband

and a wife. While some marriages in Old Testament days were arranged, there is no questioning the fact that by the time Paul wrote the epistles, he was certain that no matter how a couple came together, love—a deep commitment to care—was the glue that was not only possible but necessary to hold a relationship together.

Insight

Because God is love we who are His children love as well, and the closer we are to Him the greater will be our love for each other.

In the New Testament, both husbands and wives are told to love each other. Paul says specifically, "Husbands, love your wives, just as Christ loved the church and gave himself up for her to make her holy, cleansing her by the washing with water through the word" (Ephesians 5:25-26). Again, when Paul wrote to Titus, a young man who was a pastor and overseer in the church, he instructed that older women were to teach "the younger women to love their husbands and children" (Titus 2:4). Whether or not romantic love was the spark which led to marriage, it is obvious that the spark of love can be ignited and love can become the chemistry that makes relationships vibrant and meaningful.

In tennis, love means nothing—in marriage it means everything. It is God's answer to the loneliness of the human heart and the door to meaningful relationships.

Think on This

1. Take time to study Ephesians 5, beginning with verse 18. Note that Paul commands husbands to love their

wives as Christ loved the church. Do you consider this to be a kind of "benchmark" to shoot at or something which can actually be achieved? Do you think that God ever asks us to do the impossible?

2. In the book of Ruth (which is your resource reading for today), there is a beautiful story of commitment. How does this speak to your heart?

Resource Reading
Ruth 1–2

Wisdom, Knowledge and Understanding

"If any of you lacks wisdom, he should ask God, who gives generously to all without finding fault, and it will be given to him." (James 1:5)

Nearly half of all marriages the world over are ending in failure, and of those which endure, many are relationships of convenience where happiness eludes those who stick it out.

Long ago, the writer of Proverbs penned these words: "By wisdom a house is built, and through understanding it is established; through knowledge its rooms are filled with rare and beautiful treasures" (Proverbs 24:3-4). Solomon, the probable author of Proverbs, had experience in both good and bad relationships and in construction and building. He stresses three qualities in this passage: wisdom, understanding and knowledge. Solomon suggests that all three of these are necessary to build the home—and marriage—that endures the storm.

First is the need for wisdom in choosing the right person. Equally important is *being* the right person. As I'm writing today's thoughts, I'm in the Ukraine where my wife and I have been teaching a two-week course about family living at the Donetsk Christian University. "How can I be sure to pick the right person?" some of the students have been asking, as though by some means such as when you thump a watermelon or pinch a loaf of bread to see if it is fresh, you could be sure to pick the right one.

The New Testament book of James says, "If any of you lacks wisdom, he should ask God, who gives generously to all without finding fault, and it will be given to him" (1:5). He can give us wisdom about anything—even learning to cope with existing marriages and relationships.

A final thought regarding wisdom. Today we have more information than wisdom. The amount of knowledge available to a person has proliferated in recent years, almost in direct proportion to the growth of the Internet and our ability to store and retrieve data. But sadly the wisdom which utilizes the knowledge we have is still in short supply. Some of the world's most brilliant individuals, lacking wisdom, have ruined their lives and marriages, ending their years in bitterness and disillusionment.

> W*isdom, understanding and knowledge are necessary to build the home—and marriage—that endures the storm.*

The second quality which the Proverbs writer stresses in this passage is understanding. Interestingly enough the Hebrew word in the Old Testament usually translated "to understand" also means "to listen." Wise is the mom or dad—or any person—who is quick to pick up on the nonverbal signals that people send and who develops a listening ear. Wise is the husband who understands there are times when a wife needs flowers and times when she needs to be offered a helping hand.

The third quality the writer of Proverbs mentions is knowledge of what to bring into your home. "Through knowledge," he says, the rooms of this house "are filled with rare and beautiful treasures." What do you treasure? Does your list of treasures include memories, pleasures, experiences together, laughter and joy? Or is yours a house filled with antiques and exquisite paintings, giving it more of the appearance of a museum or art gallery than a house where people live?

Insight

Stuart Hamblin, the cowboy singer, used to say that it takes a heap of livin' to make a house a home. More sophisticated was the assessment of an unknown author who said, "A house is made of wood and beams but a home is made of love and dreams." Both are right.

Give me a house any day with a lived-in look that includes a few fingerprints on the walls, a few dirty dishes in the sink, a few kids' toys littering the floor and the ring of laughter and happiness, rather than a house which is antiseptically neat with everything in its place but love. Solomon was right: "By wisdom a house is built, and through understanding it is established; through knowledge its rooms are filled with rare and beautiful treasures" (Proverbs 24:3-4).

Think on This

1. When you face difficult situations or hard decisions, ask God for wisdom (James 1:5); then proceed carefully.

2. Wise is the person who prays before any decision. Then if you are still in doubt and have to make a decision, seek the counsel of an older, godly person whom you respect.

Resource Reading
Proverbs 24

When Disagreements Come

"Be kind and compassionate to one another, for-giving each other, just as in Christ God forgave you." (Ephesians 4:32)

No marriage was ever destroyed by conflict, but a multitude of them are destroyed every year by a refusal to *resolve* conflict. There's a difference! Conflict in marriage is part of life; it's the result of two people coming together from different backgrounds, bringing with them different habit patterns and attitudes.

No matter how you love someone, no matter how deeply committed to that person you may be, and, no matter how fervent you are in your commitment to doing the will of God, you are going to face conflict in marriage!

In spite of the fact that more marriages are failing than ever before, the fact remains that what is tearing us apart today is the same thing which destroyed families centuries ago. Proof? The pages of the book of Genesis! Read what Moses wrote and see the same problems facing families today—infidelity, conflict of values, battles over "rights," jealousy, rivalry between brothers and dishonesty with each other.

Any couple serious about saving a marriage must learn how to resolve issues before those issues destroy their relationship. Mary Ann Castronovo Fusco, a journalist and mother of two, learned that lesson. She said, "My husband and I have been married for nine years and have lots of arguments. But we love each other, and we're both committed to our relationship. You have to be willing to work at stability."

The following are guidelines to resolving conflict which could save your marriage. They work if you are willing to make them work.

A*ny couple serious about saving their marriage must learn how to resolve issues before those issues destroy their relationship.*

Guideline #1: Try to understand the person with whom you have conflict. This means you don't scream or yell at the person. You don't call him or her names. You mentally cross the room and ask, "How would I view this situation if I were in his shoes?" Psychologists call it role playing. Christians call it the golden rule. I call it the first step to a solution which can save your marriage.

Guideline #2: Pray about the conflict which causes you annoyance and irritation. Prayer changes things, right? Wrong! Prayer changes people and people change things. Prayer is a therapy which allows you to vent your anger in a positive way. It also helps you see your own inadequacies and failures. It humbles you as you bow before God and realize you are also human and subject to failure. It plugs you into God's current. Jesus put it, "Ask and you will receive, and your joy will be complete" (John 16:24).

Guideline #3: Confront the individual with whom you have conflict. We often think of confrontation as being negative. Actually, it's positive—when done in the right way. It allows an emotional wound to be cleansed and drained so healing can take place. Choose the time, the manner and the place of confrontation. When you confront someone be positive. Instead of saying, "YOU did this . . ." try saying, "This is how I feel when you do this . . ." Jesus said, "If your brother [or husband, or wife] sins against you, go and show him his fault, just between the two of you" (Matthew 18:15).

Insight

Conflict never destroys relationships. It's our refusal to resolve conflict which tears us apart.

Guideline #4: Be quick to forgive. Bitterness is a cancer that destroys *you*—not the other person. Apply a big dose of Ephesians 4:32 which says, "Be kind and compassionate to one another, forgiving each other."

Guideline #5: Bury the issue and get on with your life and relationship. There is always risk attached to love, but without love there can be no future for a marriage. Resolving conflict only strengthens marriage. Work at it; it pays big dividends.

Think on This

1. Be the first to move toward the peace table, realizing that there is far more to be gained by resolution than by holding on to your bitterness.

2. Do you agree that hatred is like taking poison and waiting for the other person to die? If so, why do you hold on to angry, harsh feelings?
3. Is there someone in your life with whom you have had a disagreement? If so, are you willing to put into practice the simple but effective guidelines listed on the preceding pages?

Resource Reading
James 4:1-10

Regular Maintenance Required

*"Accept one another, then, just as Christ ac-
cepted you, in order to bring praise to God."*
(Romans 15:7)

If people did no more maintenance on their automobiles than they do on their marriages, they would be
walking—not driving. Their cars would be broken down
with blown gaskets, burned valves and flat tires.

Marriage requires maintenance! The following are ten
guidelines of marriage maintenance which produce rich
rewards.

Guideline #1: Insist that the other *always* be first.
Selfishness—"Me first!"—does more to draw lines and
create conflict than just about anything else. Healthy relationships require that each person have an attitude of
generosity as opposed to selfishness. When a person becomes infected with the "I want mine first" mentality, a
marriage is headed for trouble.

Guideline #2: Don't sleep on conflict. This, of course, could mean that you may go for several nights without a wink of sleep! Conflict doesn't go away by sleeping on it. Avoiding talking through issues only compounds the problem. Make it a rule never to go to sleep until what is bothering you has been resolved.

Guideline #3: Always boost the other person. Some couples love each other yet allow sarcasm and sharp barbs to slip into their conversation. Some intentionally belittle their mates to make them look bad. Not a good idea! It actually makes *you* look bad, not your spouse, because you're the one who married that person.

If people did no more maintenance on their automobiles than they do on their marriages, they would be walking—not driving.

Guideline #4: Pray together every day. If I were to single out one very powerful habit which has made a difference with my marriage, it would be the importance of grasping hands and opening our hearts to our heavenly Father on a daily basis. Prayer takes the edge off. It makes us back away from insisting on our point of view as we say, "Thy will be done!"

Guideline #5: Don't insist on winning every round. In a real sense, marriage is an ongoing series of compromises involving "give and take," not "I give and you take!"

Guideline #6: Give your mate the freedom to be his or her own person. Marriage should enrich and enhance the other person as a beautiful setting does a diamond. How is this done? Encourage the other person to develop gifts and talents. Compliment each other. Be sincere and genuine. A husband or a wife has more to do with the success or failure of their spouse than anyone else in the world.

Guideline #7: Love your mate "as is," without nagging or correction. Love them as they are with the expectancy that God will make them what they ought to be!

Guideline #8: Be the first to say, "I'm sorry, forgive me!" Even if you feel like screaming, "But it wasn't my fault!" it is best to be the first to ask for forgiveness. In the long run, it doesn't matter whose fault something was; all that matters is that a problem needs healing. So take the first step.

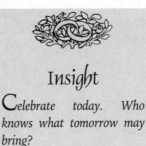

Insight

Celebrate today. Who knows what tomorrow may bring?

Guideline #9: Work on yourself first. Some folks work so hard making over the person they married they don't have time to be very good husbands or wives themselves.

Guideline #10: Enjoy today, for it is the only moment which is really yours. Who knows what tomorrow may hold? Enjoy that cup of coffee together, the walk at sunset, the smile of your grandchildren. It's the moment God has given to you. Live it to the fullest.

Think on This

1. Take paper and pencil and use these ten guidelines as a checklist against which you measure yourself. Which ones do you need to work on?
2. Since you can't start *over* (there is no going back to "Square One" on the game board of life), you can start

again, today. Why not? The past need not be a hindrance to the future.

Resource Reading
Matthew 7:24-27

Afterword

We've finally come to the end, but hopefully the end of this book is but the beginning of a new relationship with your spouse. "I have lived with the constant expectation that things will be better tomorrow," one man said at his fiftieth anniversary. He was more of an optimist than a lot of folks; nonetheless, God can be the difference in your relationship.

If you need to get professional help, I would encourage you to seek out a pastor or counselor who will keep your confidence, has his own act together and can help you and your mate work out your differences.

Anybody can quit but those who persist, who don't give up at the first sign of a cloud on the horizon, are almost always very glad that they persisted. One of my heroes is a New Zealander who, along with his Sherpa guide Norgay Tensing, climbed Mt. Everest for the first time: Sir Edmund Hillary. When he was asked why he succeeded when others failed, he said that he just took one more step. And that was enough to let him stand where no other person had ever stood before.

It works the same way in marriage.

Two questions that I hope you will focus on are these: "What are we going to do differently as the result of working through the selections in this book? What would God have us to do?" Then, do what your heart tells you.

Since 1963, I have been broadcasting—presently over a network of over 600 radio stations—and I have yet to hear from a person who can honestly say, "As a couple we went to church together, read our Bibles on a daily basis and prayed together and still our marriage failed!" Nor do I expect to hear from anyone who can honestly say that in the future. But I have heard from thousands who said with remorse, "We used to do that," and they often add with nostalgia, "Those were some of the best days of our lives."

I was driving down the freeway in my little red pickup on my way to speak at a church on Sunday morning, happy as a lark. I was listening to beautiful music and thinking what a blessing it was to be alive. Then I felt something warm on my pant leg and sock. I looked down to see the large mug of coffee I had lying on its side, empty. Driving with one hand, I grabbed a rag I had under the seat and began to daub at my pant leg and shoe which had caught part of the spilled coffee.

Then I look up and realized that in the confusion I had missed my turnoff. Quickly I jammed on the brakes only to realize that there was no way I could back up five miles on a California freeway to take the turnoff. So then I had to ask myself, "How can I get to where I want to go from where I am?"

That's the issue that confronts you as well. You can't go back, but you can go forward, *connecting* with each other and with God, deciding where you want to go with your marriage and how you can get there.

I would be glad to hear from you personally. You are also invited to visit our web site for resource materials that can help you in your personal life and marriage.

You can write to me in the United States at:

Dr. Harold Sala
Box G
Laguna Hills, CA 92677
www.guidelines.org
E-mail:guidelines@guidelines.org

In Asia write to:
Dr. Harold Sala
Box 4000
1284 Makati City
Philippines
E-mail: guidphil@compass.com.ph

Endnotes

1. James Wharton as quoted by James Jewett in *Illustrations Unlimited* (Wheaton, IL: Tyndale House, 1988), p. 335.

2. "Most Married, but Little Missed," *Los Angeles Times*, July 19, 1997, pp. A-1, 19.

3. Ibid.

4. Robin Fields, "Unwed Partners Up 72% in U.S.," *Los Angeles Times*, August 20, 2001, p. A-13.

5. The Associated Press, September 3, 1992, as quoted by "Divorce rates higher for those who shack up," *The American Family Association Journal*, February, 1993, p. 15.

6. George Gallup as quoted by Michael J. McManus in *National and International Religion Report*, "Churches: Wedding Factories or Marriage Savers?" (Roanoke, VA: Media Management, 1993), p. 1.

7. "Is Divorce Really the Answer?" *Women's Day*, September 21, 1993, p. 52.

8. Franklin Adams as quoted by Zenith Gross in *Seasons of the Heart*, (Novato, CA: New World Library, 2000), p. 144.

9. Lewis Carroll, *Alice's Adventures in Wonderland* as quoted by George Sweeting, *Who Said That?* (Chicago: Moody Press, 1995), p. 307.

10. "He Might Hang Again to Write 'I Love You' " *The Register*, July 5, 1978, A-5.

11. C.S. Lewis, *Mere Christianity* (New York: Macmillan Company, 1969), p. 99.

12. Story taken from *The Vow* by Kim and Krickitt Carpenter (Nashville, TN: Broadman and Holman Publishers, 2000).

13. Zig Zigler, *Raising Positive Kids in a Negative World* (New York: Balentine Books, 1989), p. 128.

14. From *Tomorrow Starts Today* by Harold J. Sala (Uhrichsville, OH: Barbour Publishers), June 26 selection, used by permission of Barbour Publishers, Box 719, Uhrichsville, OH 44683.

15. *Orange County Register*, June 17, 1998, p. 20.

16. From *Tomorrow Starts Today* by Harold J. Sala (Uhrichsville, OH: Barbour Publishers), June 17 selection, used by permission of Barbour Publishers, Box 719, Uhrichsville, OH 44683.

17. James Hewett, *Illustrations Unlimited* (Wheaton: Tyndale House, 1988), p. 330.

18. From *Tomorrow Starts Today* by Harold J. Sala (Uhrichsville, OH: Barbour Publishers), September 11 selection, used by permission of Barbour Publishers, Box 719, Uhrichsville, OH 44683.

19. Annette Lawson, "All About Adultery," *Bottom Line*, February 15, 1990, p. 14.

20. James Hassett, "But That Would Be Wrong," *Psychology Today*, November 1981, p. 34.

21. *New Bible Commentary Revised*, p. 483.

22. James Hassett, "But That Would Be Wrong," *Psychology Today*, November 1981, p. 37.

23. Randolph Schmidt, "Unwed Couples Living Together: Number Soars," *Orange County Register*, September 16, 1985, p. 3.

24. James Hewett, p. 331.

25. Deborah Tannen, "Why Can't He Hear What I'm Saying?" *McCall's*, January 1985, pp. 20-24.

26. Louis Sahagun, "Many Say They Knew It All Along," *Los Angeles Times*, November 29, 2000, pp. 1, 18-20.

27. Joyce Brothers, "Men and Women—The Differences," *Women's Day*, February 9, 1982, p. 140.

28. Ibid.

29. Joyce Brothers, "Men and Women—The Differences," from *What Every Woman Should Know About Men* as excerpted in *Woman's Day*, February 9, 1982, p. 138.

30. John Laragh, *Woman's Day*, February 9, 1982, p. 140.

31. Merle Shain, *Courage My Love*, as quoted in "Points to Ponder," *Reader's Digest*, March, 1991, p. 162.

32. Carl Rogers as quoted by George Sweeting in *Who Said That?* (Chicago: Moody Press, 1995), p. 338.

33. From *Tomorrow Starts Today* by Harold J. Sala (Uhrichsville, OH: Barbour Publishers) February 13 selection, used by permission of Barbour Publishers, Box 719, Uhrichsville, OH 44683.

34. From *Tomorrow Starts Today* by Harold J. Sala (Uhrichsville, OH: Barbour Publishers) February 14 selection, used by permission of Barbour Publishers, Box 719, Uhrichsville, OH 44683.

35. Gary Chapman, *The Five Love Languages* (Northfield, MS: Northfield Publishing, 1992), n.p.

36. Stephen Carter as quoted by Dennis Rainey, "Two-Minute Offense," *Life@Work*, January/February 2000, p. 10. Used by permission.

37. Ibid.

38. McManus, *National and International Religion Report*, p. 1.

39. Online: http://www.barna.org/cgi-bin/PageCategory.asp?CategoryID=20.

40. John Bunyan as quoted in *Prayer Powerpoints* by Randall Roth (Wheaton, IL: Victor Books, 1995), p. 58.

41. Gene Edward Veith, "Doing Without Marriage," *World*, April 29, 2000, p. 25.

42. Carol J. Williams as quoted by Gene Edward Veith, "Doing Without Marriage," *World*, April 29, 2000, p. 29.

43. Gary Chapman, *Five Signs of a Loving Family* (Chicago: Moody Press, 1997), p. 168.

44. Ambrose Bierce as quoted by Howard Whitman, "Love after 10 Years of Marriage," *Greenville Piedmont*, October 5, 1964, p. 7.

45. Gallup Poll and National Opinion Research (Prayer Therapy and Marriage).

46. Vernon Grounds, *The Navigators Log*, January 1970, p. 7.

47. David Gelman with Paul Kandell, "Isn't It Romantic?" *Newsweek*, January 18, 1993, p. 60.

48. Ibid.

Also by Harold Sala:

Joyfully Single in a Couple's World

Touching God: 52 Guidelines for Personal Prayer

*Raising Godly Kids: 52 Guidelines
for Counter-Culture Parenting*

*Heroes—People Who Have Made
a Difference in Our World*

Tomorrow Starts Today

How to Be Ready When Friends Ask for Help

Tomorrow Can Be Beautiful

Winning Your Inner Struggles